Observing the Class
Observing the Children

Waldorf Journal Project #18

Compiled and edited by
DAVID MITCHELL

If you want your children to be intelligent, read them fairy tales. If you want them to be geniuses, read them more fairy tales. When I examine myself and my methods of thought, I come to the conclusion that the gift of fantasy has meant more to me than any talent for abstract, positive thinking.

– Albert Einstein

Printed with support from the Waldorf Curriculum Fund

Published by:

Waldorf Publications at the
Research Institute for Waldorf Education
38 Main Street
Chatham, NY 12037

Waldorf Journal Project #18
Title: *Observing the Class, Observing the Children*
Editor: David Mitchell
Translators: Genie Sakaguchi, Ted Warren
Layout: Ann Erwin
© 2011 by AWSNA Publications, reprinted 2015
ISBN #9781-936367-83-2

Cover painting by a Waldorf student from Boulder, Colorado
Interior illustrations: Waldorf students in North America

Contents

5   Foreword

7   The Art of Observing Children
Christof Wiechert

12   What Does a Good Child Observation Entail?
Klaus Hadamovsky

16   What Is a Child Observation? [Child Study]
Anna Seydel

22   Different Children – Different Childhood
Armin Krenz

29   Born as an Original – Died as a Copy
Henning Köhler

31   Love Melts Away Fear
Henning Köhler

33   The Secret of Children's Drawings
Armin Krenz

38   Normal Is the Difference: Maxims for Successful Integration
Henning Köhler

46   Anything but Children's Play: What Play in School Means for Learning
Irene Jung

51   Love Enables Knowledge
Lorenzo Ravagli

Contents

54   Methods before Age Nine
Ted Warren

84   What Was That? Forgetting and Remembering
Albert Schmelzer

91   Brought to School by the Police?
Henning Köhler

93   Elemental Beings Are Real for Many Children
Conversation with Katharina Dreher-Thiel

96   Laughing with the Ninth Grade – Humor in the Main Lesson
Florian Heinzmann

Foreword

The *Waldorf Journal Project,* sponsored by the Waldorf Curriculum Fund, brings translations of essays, magazine articles, and specialized studies from around the world to English-speaking audiences. This eighteenth edition can be said to generally follow the theme of child observation and class observation. Most appeared originally in the German periodical *Erziehungkunst*, the Swedish magazine *På Skole* or the Norwegian journal *Steinerskolen*.

We hope that this *Journal* will help teachers and others gain insight into the seeds of Waldorf education. For those not interested in downloading the material, spiral bound copies are available from:

Waldorf Publications
38 Main Street
Chatham, NY 12037

by phone at: 518/634-2222
or by e-mail at: robin@waldorf-research.org

The editor, David Mitchell, was interested in receiving your comments on the material for this publication during his lifetime. We at Waldorf Publications are interested, in the spirit of his limitless interest in research from the field and in the news, in hearing from you. We would also be interested in hearing what areas you would like to see represented in future *Journal* projects. If you know of specific articles that you would like to see translated, please contact Waldorf Publications.

– The Editorial Staff
Waldorf Journal Projects

The Art of Observing Children

by Christof Wiechert
translated by Genie Sakaguchi

Is it possible to learn the art of child—or student—observation? There are two answers: yes and no. Yes, as a human being can learn everything. No, because one can never be finished with learning it. As soon as one believes one can do it, one is in a risky situation, comparable to an artist who is completely relaxed before a concert, feeling he is already able to do it. Either it is successful, or it is nothing. It is also like this in the case of a child study. One never knows whether it will be successful; one is rather tense, as when one has stage fright. Will we really be able to recognize this child in his true being and, through that, be able to help him?

Conditions for a child study

An essential feature of this art is that it takes place in a community. A colleague has a question about a student. The student doesn't respond as expected, or doesn't achieve what the teacher had hoped for him. The teacher would like to understand the student, for he realizes that without this understanding, he will not be able to reach the student, and learning will become difficult. He knows: *Education requires relationship*. So he turns to his colleagues and asks for guidance. The faculty meeting actually has no more important work than to enable these mutual discussions on pedagogical matters. What is necessary for such a conversation to be successful?

1. There must be a community, a circle *without gaps*. If a person is not interested in this work, it would be better for him to stay away. If a person cannot feel sympathy towards the student, he should stay out of the circle. For the conversation depends on the active interest of all participants; it is *the high school of interest*. Thus the parents can take part as well as colleagues who do not know the student. Through their neutral interest they can bring up important questions. It is helpful when the colleague who is presenting the student does not also have to chair the conversation.

2. A child study requires *breathing*. Once one has practiced this art for a while, one will need at least an hour. It makes a difference who belongs to the circle. The true activity lies not so much in the presentation by the colleague but rather in the quality of *listening*. Where does one perceive what light begins to bring into the darkness of the events portrayed? When do the described situations begin to speak, bringing light for understanding the child?

3. An important condition is a situation of peace in the social life. These are lofty words that one does not use or like to hear very often any more. However, they are true. A College that has been damaged from debates over structure or similar problems will not easily find itself ready for a child study—for the child study needs a certain *mood*. A conversation that consists only of reports and information will not be able to bring about such a mood.

4. At the end of the conversation, the group should strive to come to an agreement on one or more supports for the student. After eight weeks or so following the child study, the group can look back and ask the question: Have we done what we agreed to do and has it helped? If this can take place, the child study will become one of the strongest instruments to ensure the real quality of the school. In this activity, the College not only helps the child, but it also learns a very great deal. Many complain that Rudolf Steiner's *Study of Man** is just theory. But [in practicing this method of] child study, the study of man becomes really *practical*. Whoever participates in these conversations can feel them to be a *fortunate experience* [*Glückserlebnis*].

5. Basically there is no given model or protocol for a child study. In this work, the priorities are set by the child himself, as he becomes recognized. However, one can differentiate three stages. These have existed since the time of Hippocrates: *Anamnese* (medical history), *Diagnose* (diagnosis), and *Therapie* (therapy). In the case of a child study, we can speak of *description* or *characterization*, of *understanding*, and of *help or support*, which would be found through intuition, through the process of the child study.

Speaking and listening – inclusive

The class teacher or class sponsor presents the student as he experiences him, as the student presents himself. The teacher tries to describe the student's physical characteristics, features, and behavior, and shows examples of his work: in short, builds a picture of the student. This also includes a developmental picture of the student over time [*Zeitgestalt*]. The picture is expanded by other colleagues. If possible, the school doctor will bring any relevant history of the student. Those who are presenting the student practice the art of *inclusive speaking*, and the others practice the art of *inclusive listening*, listening not only with the ears, but also with the heart. The one who is presenting is furnishing building stones for discovery of the truth; he should not speak out of long pent-up frustrations of the soul. Naturally, this part often goes on too long. Everyone has something to say, even if one says the same thing as the person who spoke before. It is the only opportunity for one to speak out of experience, but one need not know everything.

A feeling for evidence arises.

Now it becomes conspicuously quiet in the room. Who has something to say? Who is able to interpret the picture [of the child] appropriately? Here it becomes evident how far the members of a College have been able to make [Steiner's] study of the human being their own. For an interpretation or understanding arises out of this way of understanding a human being. The person who speaks merely of what he has read has a different effect than the person who has taken the study of man* into his own inner understanding. Here one must have a feeling of colleagueship that is capable of recognizing

---

*Translator's note: Readers familiar with Steiner's pedagogical writings will know that *Allgemeine Menschenkunde* is a specific book, published in English as *Study of Man*, also under the title *Foundations of Human Experience*. But there are other places in this article where the author refers to Steiner's *Menschenkunde*. This can mean the particular book, but it could also refer to many other instances in Steiner's writings where he expands on the nature of the human being. In these cases, I have used "study of man" with lower case letters.

the capacities of one's colleagues. Listening and holding oneself back are both necessary. A refined sense for the evidence [indications] will arise: what is coherent, what is not.

Rudolf Steiner gave many indications for such interpretations that a College should work through in its meetings. According to my view, Steiner's study of man provides everything one needs to understand even the phenomena of today. In the course of the conversation, this is also the right moment to ask oneself with empathy: How would I feel if I were described in this way? How does it feel to experience from within the urge to impetuous movement, for example? How about stuttering? Or dyslexia? Such questions can help overcome shortcomings in one's general understanding of the study of man, but they should not become an end in itself. The person who listens carefully will notice that the child, the student is gradually revealed.

The most decisive thing is the will to help.

And how do we help now? To begin with, we look for means of support among the *teachers* and the *pedagogy*. After that it can be determined whether or not specialized help is needed. What kind of *subject matter* helps with which kinds of problems? What effect does math have on a student? What about drawing or even form drawing? How does a foreign language work on a child? What about stronger intellectual demands, or perhaps a more picture-like approach? What [kind of effect does one find] with musical activities or with graphic or plastic arts? Could the child be supported with exercises that work on building the memory or though speech exercises? The possibilities are legion. Rudolf Steiner said: *Education, instruction is gentle healing*. Here the will to help has a greater effect than the correct point of view. In essence we are all helpless, and can only try to prepare ourselves to be helpful. The child study concludes with the determination of who will do what for the child. After eight or ten weeks there should be a review, asking: Have we done what we agreed to do and has it had an effect?

Parent participation – a question of tact

Following a basic ethical feeling, one would seek, as far as possible for the parents' consent for the child study, and one would say why one believes it is advisable. *In principle there is nothing* against the parents participating in the child study, if they so wish. However the College of Teachers should ask itself whether the relationship between the parents and the school would support or allow this participation. The answer is a matter of tact, not of principle. And tact is generally healthy human understanding with feeling.

The child or student study is a quality instrument which, wisely used, has no equal.

About the author: Christof Wiechert is a former Head of the Pedagogical Section at the Goetheanum. His book, *Lust aufs Lehrersein (Desire to Become a Teacher),* has recently been published by the Goetheanum Press.

What Does a Good Child Observation Entail?

by Klaus Hadamovsky
translated by Genie Sakaguchi

Without time, quiet, and undivided attention, the individuality of the child cannot be illuminated in a child observation [child study]. Even the school doctor must set aside his professional side in the conversation.

If I feel the child study has been successful, when I leave with two experiences: First of all, with an actual spiritual experience, which cannot be proven, but is so concrete that any discussion would be moot. Something has taken place between me and the spiritual individuality of the child whose being was illuminated in the child study; soul contact has been made that gives me a joyful lift. Secondly, surprising new ideas emerge for the aid, treatment, and possibly further diagnosis for this child.

In my opinion, whether or not a College of Teachers thrives depends on these two experiences. If the College shares such experiences, then it grows together, is able to nourish itself in a soul-spiritual way, and can resist burnout. When the math teacher, a professed agnostic and a formidable cynic, declares with sparkling eyes after the child study that he has just had an idea of how he can now approach the youth who has been the subject of their conversation—this good man has had a flash of inspiration, an intuition, whatever he might call it in his own words, and he has participated in the process.

To be able to have a meaningful part in a child study there are, however, certain obstacles to be overcome. The most difficult obstacles are erected by the participants themselves, when they come to the meeting with opinions or with subjective judgments that they would like to exchange and have confirmed. It is not about these opinions, but rather the child study has to do with something completely new. Many participants express a lack of interest as well as a lack of discipline because they have no relationship to the child under observation. Lack of interest and lack of discipline are two aspects of subjectivity that can disrupt any group process.

Really join in or leave the room.

In order for something new to arise, all such subjective things must be overcome. Opinions are old, subjective judgments that one brings along. Even if they have just come up in the last few minutes, they stand in the way of what is truly new. These opinions will be most easily overcome when one makes for oneself a comprehensive picture of the child. The comprehensiveness of this picture can be achieved only by the College of Teachers as a whole, for individuals lack the perceptions and perspective of the other members.

Whoever is not concerned or involved in the process must involve himself, that is, develop an interest in and attention for the child or he should leave the room. A sermon in a church might perhaps continue even if someone is snoring in the first pew, but a child study cannot endure if someone snoozes, whispers, or only quietly corrects notebooks. It is like many other accomplishments in our culture: A single person cannot bring it about, but he can definitely disturb it.

Whether the picture of the child becomes so clear that it attains illuminating power and allows the spiritual individuality of the child to be glimpsed depends on the working together of all those present. After many decades of participating in such presentations, I have asked myself if this way of working really lends itself to a College of 30, 40, or 50 teachers, or if it is more often a matter of good luck when it happens to be successful.

Under the pressure of time, the big talkers assert themselves.

Perhaps the most unpleasant disturbances arise from the subjective experience of being pressed for time. Most teachers of both genders express the feeling that they have no time; there are always an endless number of things to be done in every school! At the same time, there is nothing more important than what is happening now, in this moment.

Only in light of a completely newly-developed perceptive picture can one come to any judgment of the child, and to start looking for solutions, from which all concerned might expect something new. This also requires time and peace. Under the pressure of time, the most brilliant speakers immediately assert themselves, the most ingenious characterizers and interpreters of children's capacities and parents' faults. Perceptions of the child under consideration cannot be expressed. The participants go home with information instead of an intuition. Meetings of class teachers or subject teachers, in which smaller numbers of teaching staff who are directly involved, might more easily find their way to this goal, if they give themselves enough time to work methodically, and not merely exchange opinions.

The combination of medical-therapeutic and pedagogical points of view in the child study is only fruitful, in my estimation, when these two experiences come about: the inmost contact with the individuality of the child and the intuition for completely new ideas. If these things do not happen, one [the doctor] remains in the realm of one's know-how, gives tips and information of a medical nature, but nothing that could really change a life.

The parents also need intuition.

It also happens often that a successful child study ends up in bitter disappointment. As a teacher or doctor, one would like to discuss the results with the parents—and [then] they do not go along with it! They are not able to agree, because one has simply given them the new insights, instead of helping them to find their own way to these ideas. [When we do this] the parents miss out on the process which could release them from their own subjectivity in their hour of need—for when do child studies take place otherwise?—the process that could have helped them come to intuitions, to be ready for unprecedented new ideas about their child and, above all, for impulses for action. [That being said], should one involve the parents in the child study? Nonsense! All the participants would be overwhelmed. These conversations live within the methodical discipline and competence of the participants, and require intimacy; I hope I have clearly expressed this.

This dilemma can be solved when one arranges "helping discussions," round-table discussions to which all are invited who feel themselves directly involved with this child: parents, class teachers, the school doctor, perhaps certain subject teachers, perhaps also other family members and therapeutic professionals from within as well as outside the school. The parents stand in the middle of this conversation, and they decide, with the class teacher and school doctor, whom they would like to have present.

A father sees himself.

Usually the conversation circle consists of five to seven participants, who work amazingly efficiently together. Basically it is a spontaneously arranged spiritual-pedagogical self-help group. Since the participants are not used to working together, they need to take more time to create a picture, approximately ten minutes per person. The total time required to create the picture, work towards an understanding, come to the closing phase and a looking back over what has been experienced, would be at least ninety minutes. For all steps the group should observe the proven ground rules for all self-help groups. First of all: no questions; secondly: no advice.

Finally [it is recognized that] the parents are more involved than all the rest of the participants, and they rightfully react with sensitivity to those instances where the limits are crossed through leading or probing questions, as well as pedagogical advice. If one does not overwhelm them with incomprehensible vocabulary, all parents are actually more spiritually open and resilient than one might expect. One time a father, a hardcore car salesman in a high-end market, declared with moist eyes after a session that the whole time he had seen himself as a young boy in this case. He has had his intuition. … Whatever he calls it, it will have beneficial results. To be sure, such round-table conversations are time-consuming and are not necessary for every child. But in many problem cases they prove to be worthwhile, and it does not really matter whether the problem is located with the child or with other participating adults.

About the author: Klaus Hadamovsky is a school doctor at the Flensburg Waldorf School. As a general practitioner he conducts, with his wife, a medical-pedagogical practice for developmental help and therapy in Flensburg.

What Is a Child Observation? [Child Study]

by Anna Seydel
translated by Genie Sakaguchi

The following article is a conversation between Anna Seydel and a writer from the journal Erziehungskunst.

Interviewer: Even those who seldom read *Erziehungskunst* will probably be aware that child observation has been practiced in Waldorf schools for quite some time. What actually is a child study?

Anna Seydel: A group of people who would like to turn their attention towards the being of a child in order to understand him. One starts by sharing impressions one has of the child with each other. As a rule the group takes up children who have developmental delays or disturbances, or who have a negative effect on the class work. These are the outer causes, to begin with. The group can also consider children who do not exhibit such noticeable problems. Through working together to look at the child, the teachers clear up their personal perspectives, animosities, and reservations. All possible points of view are brought together, creating a common picture through conversation.

---

*Translator's note: The German word *Kinderbesprechung* has been translated as "child observation" in some English-speaking Waldorf schools and "child study" in others. From the description of what is intended in a *Kinderbesprechung*, one can see that the same process is meant, whichever name it is given. I have used both interchangeably in this translation.

Interviewer: Basically, every teacher works to achieve such an understanding of the children and tries to adjust his pedagogical work accordingly. Why would a child study be necessary in addition to this?

AS: To begin with, because as a general rule development no longer proceeds without problems. The outer conditions of growing up have become, to some extent, dramatically more complicated. Family relationships have also become more complicated, as well as the relationship of the teacher to himself, with the children, and with parents and colleagues. This can lead to a point where a class teacher becomes convinced that he can no longer carry a child in his class, even when other teachers and the parents might see the child quite differently. The child study offers the chance to raise observations of the child to a new level and to enliven, illuminate, and clarify the approach to the child.

Interviewer: How would one imagine a child observation?

AS: There are many forms. For example, a class teacher can describe the child to his colleagues in a faculty meeting. It is much better, however, when the other teachers can observe the child for themselves. This can happen in a classroom, with other teachers sitting in on a class, or the child can be observed on the playground. One way that has been particularly fruitful is to invite a group of students to report on something or perform something for the circle of teachers. Then each teacher has the opportunity to observe the child who will be the subject of the child study, and to see him along with students of the same age. Again and again it is astonishing to see with what liveliness, accuracy, and diversity are the perceptions brought together, often even surprising the class teacher.

Interviewer: So it starts with observation?

AS: Yes. This is followed by the attempt to put oneself in the child's shoes, to feel one's way into what one has observed in the child. Not immediately to come to interpretations or judgments, but rather to bring oneself into alignment with the child.

Interviewer: To go back to observation: What exactly is observed?

AS: Some people see more of the outer aspects of the child: the face, the head, the hands, the arms, the form and posture of the body, in other words, everything through which the child expresses himself through his body. Then there are the more habitual aspects: how a child acts, whether he participates, what kind of tendencies the child has, and which temperament. Next is the field of the soul: how the child relates to the world through his thinking, his feeling, and his will activities, how he relates to other people and to other living beings. This is also expressed in his movements and his entire demeanor. Lastly there is the realm of the will, of intentionality. For example, how does the child approach certain tasks? How does the child follow a train of thought, or on his own plan and carry out his work, step by step? A further aspect is the destiny of the child. There are significant events in one's biography that can have an effect on the rest of one's life. Details of the child's birth should also be included in these.

Interviewer: It's not only a matter of describing what one has observed, but other knowledge about the child is brought into the picture?

AS: Yes. Here the report from the parents can be a great help for the process. But it should be about what is real, not about assumptions, speculations, interpretations, or theories, but rather about observations and perceptions.

Interviewer: What is the aim of gathering all these observations and facts?

AS: That in them and through them, one can comprehend the being of the child, that which brings the elements all together. For it is the soul-spiritual being of the child that brings forth these outer factual details. Every single detail of the outer child is an expression of its being. Goethe spoke of "finding a concise point" from which the being of a phenomenon reveals the idea within the sense-perceptible interrelationship [combination, coherence].

Interviewer: When one has found this point, does one then use it to try to explain the child's characteristics and behavior?

AS: No, it is rather that one finds something through which one can instinctively feel one's way into the child. For example, one attempts to experience inwardly how it feels when one always sits with an open mouth dreaming off into the distance. Then one notices that something always emerges. This "something" is what brings one into connection with the child. One need not understand it right away. The important thing is that the teacher or the therapist must feel the condition of the child within himself.

Interviewer: So it has to do with empathy?

AS: Yes! It has to do with the experience that I can feel the child in myself, because I have something in myself that I myself can recognize, and thus I can recognize it again in the child. I can say to myself: "I recognize you, for I am you!" Through this the child tells me who he is. Insofar as I recognize the child, he comes into my understanding, into my view. He "becomes" that which I see in him. And in my perceiving, the child finally recognizes himself, feels himself to be perceived, and comes to himself.

Interviewer: Now that one has this empathy with the child, does one go further, to find measures to take or decisions to make about how to work with the child?

AS: Not right away. First, interest streams towards the child, then the child begins to express himself in me. Now I answer back, and this answer is a soul-answer, in which I bring a balance to that which I have perceived as weaknesses in the child. This answer has the intention of bringing about equilibrium for healing. One feels, for example, that a child needs more structure, or some other kind of encouragement. That is, to begin with, only an answer in the feelings. Then in conversations with colleagues, one can gradually try to find what is the actual situation. What does it mean that a child isolates himself from his surroundings? The decisive question is not what measures [need to be taken]. What is more important is the fact that the adults have turned their attention towards the child, and through their mindfulness, they awaken interest and warmth for the child. When a person meets a child after a child study, he instinctively meets him with a different inner attitude. If the child appears slack and dejected, or even hopeless, the adult would bring an inner gesture of encouragement, of uprightness towards the child. He doesn't say, "Have a little more courage," but rather in his attitude he brings encouragement and hope towards the child.

Interviewer: Apart from any therapeutic measures, then, the fact that one has directed one's consciousness towards the child has meaning?

AS: Yes. The most effective therapeutic resource that we have is the child observation itself. One does not have to ponder too long to figure out what needs to be done concretely; that happens almost automatically. One slips, so to speak [out of one's own instincts], into a therapeutic countermeasure for a perceived weakness. One can also discover many possibilities for therapeutic measures among various subjects being taught. For example, I was able to help an asthmatic child by playing the recorder with him every day, thereby helping him to breathe out more easily. After a few years he overcame his asthma.

Interviewer: How does one accompany the child further? Is there a specific period of time after which one looks at the child anew and speaks of him again?

AS: It is naturally meaningful, after a certain time, to speak in the circle in which the child has been observed, to see what has changed. And perhaps again after a year or so it would be helpful. But one can also have the experience that a child has been the subject of a child study in the second grade and then in the following years does not need further conversations. Through the child study, and the way that the teachers work with him afterwards, the child has come into a more or less harmonious relationship with himself. And that is really the point—that the individuality of the child, the soul-spiritual aspect, comes to terms with himself.

Interviewer: Are there doubts or problems connected with the child observation? After all, one is working in a very personal and intimate manner with the child.

AS: One problem lies in the fact that often one does not speak as if the child were present. One must always be conscious that every negative judgment injures the child. It is not really about positive or negative judgments, but rather that the child begins to express himself through those who are present. Many have a problem with this process of putting oneself in the other's shoes. They say, "In this I come too near the child." Actually they are afraid to stretch themselves a bit and plunge into something that makes them uneasy. When one goes through the process of inwardly following the growth of a plant, one doesn't say, "I'm getting too close to the plant." [And just as in the plant study] we are trying to explore the being of the child through the gestures of his individuality.

Interviewer: Do the parents take part in the child study?

AS: If it's possible. I am in favor of the parents being present for gathering perceptions of the child. I have had many conversations with parents in smaller groups. In a faculty meeting of 50 teachers or so, it would not be very good to invite the parents. Many [faculty members] would be strained in such a situation, as the parents have a much deeper, many-layered and more intimate relationship with the child. For these reasons they are easily offended, which we would not want to happen. I would always prefer to discuss the child with the parents alone.

Interviewer: Should the parents be informed when a child observation is taking place?

AS: Absolutely! There should be no child study without letting the parents know what we want to attempt, and how we will do it. And there should be no child observation without an in-depth report to the parents afterwards.

About the author: Anna Seydel has been a long-time class teacher and instructor at the Teachers' Seminar in München. She has recently published a book entitled *Ich bin Du – Kindererkenntnis in pädagogischer Verantwortung [I Am You – Children's Knowledge in Pedagogical Responsibility]*. Her book can be ordered from www.waldorfbuch.de.

Different Children – Changed Childhood

by Armin Krenz
translated by Genie Sakaguchi

"In earlier times everything was different!" This sentence, uttered by the author at home, was countered by his wife with a smile: "Yes, yes—in the olden days everything was made of wood, and we still had an Emperor." Certainly a great deal has changed in the living conditions of children. Armin Krenz, of the Institute for Applied Psychology and Pedagogy in Keil, takes a look at the changes.

The facts

Changes in society:

Children and young people in Germany are growing up in an increasingly aging society. Most often they have one sibling and live, more often than earlier, in a variety of family forms, in "alternative families." They are often confronted with the separation or divorce of their parents. Approximately two thirds of children between ten and fifteen have already, at an early age, been drawn into decisions significant for their biographies.

Financial situation:

More and more often and in growing numbers, mothers are gainfully employed, and almost 25 percent of the actively employed mothers in the newly formed German states have a child less than three years of age. Almost 40 percent of the women with children under fourteen work in the evenings and on Saturdays, more than one quarter work on Sunday, and 16 percent work nights.

Single parents have a significantly higher risk of living in poverty than couples with children. Poverty for children and youth has been growing steadily since the 1990s. Parents today might spend up to half of the net family household income for the children.

Changed living situation:

To a large degree daily life is institutionally structured—through caretakers, the lengthening of school-time, and a plethora of activities for free time available in the educational and cultural realms. The specialization of life activities isolates children and young people more and more away from the society of adults, at the same time that the "worlds" of adolescents are more differentiated in the course of the day and in the course of the biography.

Children and youth who grow up in or near an urban residential area with a lot of traffic have to put up with sharply diminished opportunities for experiences and development in their neighborhoods.

Shifting of educational processes:

Educational experiences have shifted increasingly into out-of-school activities. Through the very different economic situations of the parents, very significant inequalities can develop in the educational possibilities of children and young people.

Communicating with classmates, participating in cliques, watching TV or playing video games, and simple chatting with friends are the favorite free-time activities. The media are an everyday experience for many. Compared with children in other European countries, the children of Germany are the most equipped with media technology.

Different conditions of socialization lead to different childhoods.

In earlier times children could grow up within a larger, extended family, with a number of siblings, and perhaps living with the grandparents or being cared for by relatives. Today there are an increasing number of "latch-key children" who grow up in an environment shaped by technology and the media, and oriented towards consumerism. In their movements and activities they are rather limited, with extraordinarily fewer acoustical and optical impressions.

Due to career mobility the parents are either absent for the greater part of the day or existing relationships are disrupted. The increasing poverty of many families and the anxiety of searching for a job bring further insecurity into the family.

Public discussions about education have led to earlier planning for the futures of children and youth, with more and more restrictions on their available free time. On the other hand, there are parents who are not engaged in their children's education, who give little or no stimulus to their children's education. Thus peers gain more influence over the behavior and experiences of children and young people.

Material needs are being met, but not the soul needs.

All of the foregoing makes it clear that it is no longer possible to speak of a stress-free (unencumbered) childhood in Germany. Childhood as a separate, free-standing, age-appropriate life-phase is scarcely to be found anymore.

To be sure, it is easier and more possible for many children to take advantage of cognitive developmental offerings, but at the same time it becomes more difficult for them to develop physically and with emotional stability. Stable relationships give way to educational benchmarks, which entail higher behavioral expectations of children and young people. The opportunities for development, which are not as equally available when compared to previous generations, always bring along new burdens, which can be too heavy for many children and young people. This can help explain many behavioral disturbances.

Many parents fulfill the material wishes of their children more frequently than in earlier times, but in greater numbers they neglect their children's basic soul needs, which might include, for example, spending time together, giving them the gift of unstructured time, calmly accepting the child's development, letting the child feel their acceptance, granting the child space for his/her own discoveries, and giving the example of worthy guidance.

Adults involved in education can hinder the child's self-competence.

Children and young people are frequently bound up in the expectations of the nursery school, the kindergarten, the school, their parents, their neighborhood, and the cliques of friends. They lack the free space to find themselves and to learn how to experience their own competence. In earlier times one saw children as unfinished, not-yet-developed beings, but today adults who are involved in their children's education regard them as personalities with "capacities demanding cultivation." They are called serious participants, but find themselves at the same time to be in a dependent position with expectations to live up to. In this way adults contribute daily to overloading childhood with contradictions. Along these lines, they bring forth their own "picture of the child," often very inconsistently, which also leads to further disturbances for the child.

In his article, "Being a Child Is not Child's Play," Klaus Peter Brinkhoff has hit the point on the theme of "childhood today." He brings forward certain concepts about childhood:

"Airbag childhood"

Most children today are well furnished with material goods, if not extraordinarily so, and they are caught and cushioned by a predominantly functioning pedagogical (social) "airbag system."

Consumer childhood

In past generations the main concern was procuring enough food for the whole family, but now a "merciless consumption of mass-produced toys" stands in the foreground.

Media childhood

The material media furnishings of children's rooms and the extent of media usage are higher than that in any preceding generation. Children are courted and treated as consumers.

"First-row" childhood

Children witness and experience at an increasingly younger age events from which they were previously sheltered. Scenes of war and natural catastrophes are brought into the family home through television, sexuality is openly portrayed, and the "wide world" is experienced by ever-younger children through foreign travel.

Career childhood

In popular and also institutional pedagogy, many adults see "education from the very beginning" as a first principle. The greatest possible number of children should, from the earliest possible moment, find a "comfortable place on the educational carousel."

Isolated childhood

The living situation of families takes place predominantly in structured social neighborhoods. Arrangements for free time, the workplaces of the parents, shopping malls, central schools, sports fields, gyms, and outside possibilities for relaxation are more strictly separated from each other. Children are frequently transported by their parents to friends and agreed-upon places; thus continuous social contact is more and more limited.

Virtual childhood

On account of the more restricted fields of activity and more limited living spaces, children turn more often to "reality software" and "second-hand experience" as offered by the media. In the place of listening to the rustling of the trees there are nature CDs, and instead of building a tree house in the garden or the woods oneself, children avail themselves of the corresponding building game over the Internet.

Endangered childhood

The price for the continuous further development of commercialization, modernization, mechanization, industrialization, and urbanization is high. Violence and aggression among children and youth, increased psychosomatic complaints, the rise of alcohol, pill, and drug abuse, the high proportion of eating disturbances, the frequency of traffic accidents, the increase in chronic illnesses as well as both attempted and completed suicides, all disclose that children and young people are increasingly caught up in stressful situations.

Multicultural childhood

Through the recent dissolution of countries in Eastern Europe, waves of immigration and opening of the borders, Germany has become a distinctly multicultural country. Important opportunities for development have arisen through this, but cultural variety contains hidden risks as well, such as over-the-border criminal activities, human trafficking, and increased religious radicalism.

Individualized childhood

In that standards have changed quite notably, it has become more a matter of being "isolated in the masses." Traditional values lose their meaning, so that it becomes increasingly necessary for children, young people and adults to find "a new, firm ground under their feet."

Uncertain childhood

In spite of many developments in the fields of technology and medicine, children and youth are confronted with many problems. These include questions about later careers or future jobs, as well as concerns for the world climate and social questions such as providing for retirement and pensions, justice among generations, and public health.

What is missing is security in development.

One thing becomes quite clear in this list: More than ever, children need security in their development to be able to build a stable identity. We need directed observations about how children are doing in their social and emotional development, and place-specific perceptions about the actual living situations of children, to be able to find out what children need to further their individual development and which pedagogical qualities or connections help children discover their resources for development. We need to extend these effectively in everyday experiences.

Goals (consequences) for a pedagogy adapted for the present time:

- We must strongly provide for children to be allowed to be children.

- A responsible pedagogy must give attention to the specific stage of the child's development and may not be allowed to sacrifice the present for the sake of the future.

- The idea of a "perfect child" from the earliest possible moment must be given up, as childhood should be built on the idea that mistakes must be allowed to be made, from which learning can take place.

- Children need examples upon whom they model themselves.

- Instead of a strong consumers orientation, children need "nourishment for the soul" that will help them build a stable foundation for the personality.

- They are dependent on adults who will again and again take on the task of understanding them in all their varieties of expression.

- Above all else they need the feeling of security.

- They need firm attachments and reliable relationships, so that even when they fall back, they will be able to recover and meet the challenges of everyday life with confidence and commitment.

- They do not need artificially arranged living spaces, but rather, comprehensive and extensive room for play and activity, where they can have real, tangible experiences.

- They need to have enough time to process and strengthen their perceptions, to be able to understand the contexts and consequences.

- They depend on a stable self-consciousness, as they get older, to be able to take on the tasks of daily life with independence, readiness for hard work, and joy in learning.

- They need adults who will work together with optimism, joy, and devotion, to actively enter into the quest for a world where "childhood" as an independent phase of life is protected or re-established.

Let us look into ourselves, to see how much devotion, joy, courage, positive attitude towards life, and inward participation in the lives of children we can bring towards the work of the re-establishing such a worthwhile world.

LITERATURE
T. Betz: *Ungleiche Kindheiten*, Weinheim 2008.
Bundesministerium für Familie, Senioren, Frauen und Jugend (Hrsg.): 13. Kinder- und Jugendbericht, Köln 2009.
DJI – Deutsches Jugendinstitut (Hrsg.): Konsum und Umwelt im Jugend-alter, München 2009.
K. Hurrelmann: *Lebensphase Jugend*, Weinheim 2009.
A. Krenz: *Was Kinder brauchen*, Berlin 2010.

About the author: Dr. Armin Krenz works at the Institute for Applied Psychology and Pedagogy in Kiel, doing research in the field of professional development in elementary pedagogy.

Born as an Original – Died as a Copy

by Henning Köhler
translated by Ted Warren

At the end of the 1960s it was stated that a catastrophe in education had broken out and we should consider the better times in the past, in which most parents, educators and teachers acted intuitively correctly.

In the 1970s Lloyd deMause began researching the history of childhood in terms of the relationship between adults and children. The following is a short summary.

Until the 13th century, child murder was a daily event and giving away children was the rule. In the 14th century there were severe contrasts ranging from the ideal of the devoted mother (inspired by the Maria presentations in art) to the continued practice of brutal ambivalence. In the 18th century the dominating motive was to break into the core of the child's soul to rip out any immorality at its roots. "One prays with them, rather than playing with them. They were often beaten but no longer regularly whipped." (The phase of intrusion.)

From the 19th to the 20th century, the principle of socialization dominated: adjusting to the established society through education and behavior control. More subtle forms of conditioning were to make open brutality unnecessary. Yet beating children remained a socially acceptable option. "Spoiling children" became the deadly sin of education. By the 1970s the socialization model was criticized in parts of liberal society and the form of relationship called "support" was favored. According to deMause it was based on the realization that children know what is best for themselves in "every stage of their lives." He emphasizes that people are still not able to imagine education as anything other than socialization, though his book speaks of the hope for change.

The historical overview is shocking. Psychiatrist J. Louise Despert reached the same conclusions in his own studies. They brought him to the history of continual "heartlessness and cruelty." (deMause) Two things must be said about this.

The first: Today, leading educational books praise famous behaviorists from the 1930s and 1940s, such as John Watson, who published a form of the principle of conditioning as the solution to problems. They do not propose beatings but "sanctions" and other forms of punishment.

The second: In these books it is stated that by the end of the 1960s, the catastrophe in education had broken out and we should consider the better times in the past, in which most parents, educators and teachers acted intuitively correctly. If what they considered to be normal educational behavior in the 1960s was intuitively correct, then to hell with those intuitions. It was misunderstood. As long as the type of relationships are merely "supportive" and not extended to broader fronts, the words of the author Edward Young will be just as relevant as they were in the 18th century: "We are born as an original and die as a copy."

LITERATURE

Lloyd deMause, *Hort ihr die Kinder weinen. Eine psychogenetische Geschichte der Kindheit*, Frankfurt a.M., 1977.

About the author: Henning Köhler is a curative teacher, author, and director for twenty-three years of the Janusz-Korczak Institute, a curative pedagogical clinic and place for consultation on education and youth which he founded in Nürtingen, Germany. He is a lecturer at the Seminar for Waldorf Pedagogy in Cologne, Germany, and at the Institute for Pedagogy and Medicine in Verona, Italy. Twelve years ago he initiated the professional development program for consultants for specialized educational questions. Link: www.janusz-korczak-institut.de.

Love Melts Away Fear

by Henning Köhler
translated by Ted Warren

Children do not obey because parents discipline efficiently.
Whether a child obeys or not depends on the relationship.

Does it speak for or against Waldorf education that people are gathered under its roof with extremely different relationships to key questions in education? Bernard Buebs *Lob der Disziplin* [*Praising Discipline*] is very much appreciated by some Waldorf educators. Others believe in *Kinderjahre* [*The Childhood Years*] by the Swiss pediatrician Remo Largo. How does that work?

In a "taz" interview Largo was asked: "Where does the renaissance of authoritarian educational thought come from?"

Largo: "Pure nostalgia. I am convinced. The age of authoritarianism is over."

Interviewer: "But in the end children must receive some limitations."

Largo: "A typical German attitude. I have a very different opinion. Children do not obey because parents discipline efficiently. Under these circumstances education would be a nightmare. Whether a child obeys or not depends on the relationship. The same is true for their motivation for learning. There are studies about this. It is not a feel-good pedagogy."

Also Michael Winterhoff's book *Warum unsere Kinder Tyrannen werden* [*Why Our Children Become Tyrants*] has found some reception in Waldorf circles. He gets very upset about children who do not immediately follow every command with no questions asked. His credo: From early on, train the child's psyche with positive and negative reinforcement: praise and blame! Winterhoff is a "fear mogul" states Alex Ruehle in the "Süddeutsche Zeitung." Toni Feldner, who has two children just as Ruehle does, confirms the judgment in his book, *Genug erzogen* [*Educated Enough*]: "It was hard for me to read the book; one becomes very sad."

On the internet portal "We Parents," Winterhoff proclaims that before the eighth year children do not have their own personality; before the fifteenth or sixteenth year they have no insight. Largo proclaims the opposite, the individuality of the child should be respected from birth on. So thinks the brain researcher Gerald Huether, who is well-respected in Waldorf circles. Both take the side of fear-free relationships and autonomous learning. While Bueb and Winterhoff argue consequently on the level of power battles, Largo and Huether are convinced that in a good social climate, the question of power is overcome. Love melts away fear.

Miriam Gebhard writes in her book, *Die Angst vor dem kindlichen Tyrannen* [*The Fear of the Child Tyrant*]: "Whoever boldly proposes that children must learn discipline and obedience, who continually speaks of borders, must accept the fact that people remind them of the past: of all of the pope-like advisors that have contributed to German parents' fear of their child tyrants." The tyrant litany and the demand for dressage education are certainly not specific to the 20th century. They have a long and sad tradition.

Is it even meaningful to ask where Waldorf education stands historically concerning the painful themes: power, discipline and authoritarianism? Is it somewhere between the frontlines? I fear that is not possible. Mixing the colors, Bueb and Largo would give an indifferent gray-brown color, certainly not lilac. This is an invitation to debate.

The Secret of Children's Drawings

by Armin Kretz
translated by Genie Sakaguchi

Scientists around the world have tried for decades to find the meaning of pictorial expressions by human beings. In this search, they have discovered that children's drawings, in particular, show the most common features cross-culturally, both in the depiction of life experiences and in the forms of expression. The consistencies are so great that it cannot be merely coincidence that children draw "this way or that."

Whether a picture is quickly drawn in passing or drawn with great effort, whether a child carefully seeks for the right color or just grabs the first pencil that comes to hand—if one is asking about the "meaning" of children's drawings, one thing is certain: Children express their hopes, wishes, dreams, visions, and expectations in their drawings—and also their anxieties, fears, hurts, and worries. Their drawings depict their actual experienced reality—an experience of the present with a connection to the past and the future. Naturally, a child's drawing is not a consciously structured act. For this reason developmental psychologists generally do not say, "The child draws," but rather something like, "Something is being drawn by the child." In this way they refer to the feelings and inner pictures that play into the drawing process.

The "purpose" of children's drawing is simply the joy that children feel and in their wish to "express" themselves. To express themselves means to come out from under some kind of pressure. [In the German, there is a play on the words "Druck"—*pressure, stress*, and "sich ausdrücken"—*to express oneself.*] The perception of stress is not necessarily to be equated with an experience of being burdened! More often it is due to the wish of the person to free himself from feelings or thoughts, to be able to be open for new perceptions and activities.

One could also say: Children's drawings enhance and free [the child] from feelings, unburden one from thoughts that have not been worked through, and help create the possibility to be able to confront one's actual living situation with renewed forces.

First of all, one thing that is of the greatest meaning for the drawings of children has to do with the discoveries of developmental psychology: For the pictorial, graphic expression, of children there is no "right or wrong," "good or bad," acceptable or not acceptable," or "beautiful or less beautiful"! When children subjectively value and appreciate themselves and their environment—judging with emotionally charged values—then their drawings always correspond to their own imagination of what is right. Not without reason does one find in neurobiology, as well, the concept: "As a person feels, so does he think, and as he thinks, so does he act." The life of feeling shapes the direction of our thinking and brings about a corresponding pattern of behavior. In this regard there cannot and should not be an "objective correctness" for children's drawings! As children draw meaningful things larger than other things, then the depiction of a lion might be larger than that of a house or a tree. Children portray in their pictures a felt image of an actual assessment of their lives. In this sense the drawing is a stored bundle of impressions. And this is where the cultural—historical circle is closed: Impression seeks expression. Drawing joins the other five forms of expression* of children as an equally noteworthy form.

How children's drawings can be "read"

Children's drawings are always built up of six particular key elements. First of all there are the so-called "20 graphemes"—the basic signs or scribbles which range from a point to the various vertical, diagonal and horizontal lines through curves, zig-zags and wave forms to spirals, circles, and open lines. [*Grapheme* as used here does not seem to have an exact corresponding English word—*sign* or *symbol* would not be quite accurate.] Every sign (grapheme) corresponds to a specific stage of development in the first four years of life. From this, one can draw inferences about the respective developmental stage by observing how often particular signs are chosen.

In the second place we can observe the three levels of personality: competence of action, emotional competence, and cognitive competence. The drawings can show us how strongly or weakly a given area is developed. As a third step we can observe the three elements: past, present, and future. The drawings give us information about which time period the child lives in most strongly, cognitively and emotionally.

More than ninety percent of the many thousands of children's drawings that I have evaluated over the last twelve years have led me to the conclusion that children between the fourth and seventh years deal with family situations relating to the past with intensively emotional thoughts. This observation stands at cross-purposes to the cognitive, future-oriented learning demands placed on many kindergarten children today. A radical change of perspective is necessary here to prevent further hindrances for children for their long-range personality development.

The fourth element [to observe in children's drawings] arises from the choice of color. Socially-culturally oriented teachers give the highest priority of meaning to four primary and four secondary colors: red, yellow, green, and blue as well as black, white, purple, and brown. These colors play a special role in the history of mankind, and many actual findings in developmental psychology show that children use the same colors over and over again to portray their feeling-charged experiences.

Now for the fifth stage we observe the objects that are drawn, which all have a particular symbolic value assigned—mostly related to the ideas of Carl Gustav Jung. He took as his starting point the idea that every human being has in his subconscious an "enormous reservoir" that he brings with him into the world. This contains a complete set of pictures, signs, and symbols which can be activated and connected with one another through impressions from outside. Whether the drawing has to do with the sun, the stars, the moon, the clouds, a house, a particular animal, a fence, a rainbow, a forest, an explosion, a mountain or something else, these are archetypal pictures standing for particular meaningful content.

To conclude [with the sixth aspect], we would consider certain peculiarities:
- Hovering pictures, in which the people, animals, or other objects have no ground under their feet
- Pictures with a frame, in which all four sides are lined
- Doubling of objects
- The angle of inclination of tree tops or roofs of houses
- The omission of parts of objects that would be considered belonging to it
- Gluing [the picture] together, or rolling it up

Be careful with interpretation. A statement of interpretation is possible only under the following conditions:

- There must be a number of pictures on hand to compare and to check for clusters of distinctive features. Single pictures may be an image of a given day and could lead to chance generalizations.
- The basis for the interpretive work is secure knowledge.
- An overall statement would never be made from the evaluation of a few single features. It must be the result of looking at all six key aspects together.
- These statements are then only relevant when they are consistent with analyses of the other five forms of expression.*

Children's pictures are an extremely valuable document to help enable one to understand the child's environment, to discover the child's inner values, and to infer pedagogical arrangements that might be called for. We should always meet all pictures of a child with appreciation and respect, as he is entrusting us with his "soul diary."

Translator's note: In an article by Edeltraub Wiebe, "Kinder haben ein Recht darauf, verstanden zu werden! Ausdrucksformen der Kinder—sehen und verstehen" [included in the book edited by Armin Krenz, *Kindorientierte Elementarpädagogik*, Göttingen 2010, page 121], we find the six forms of children's expression: behavior, play, movement, language and speech, painting and drawing, and dreams.

LITERATURE

Armin Krenz. *Was Kinderzeichnungen erzählen. Kinder in ihrer Bildsprache verstehen*, Dortmund 2010.

Hans-Günther Richter. *Die Kinderzeichnung. Entwicklung – Interpretation – Ästhetik*, Berlin 1997.

Martin Schuster. *Kinderzeichnungen. Wie sie entstehen, was sie bedeuten*, München 2010.

Wollfgang Sehringe. *Zeichnen und Malen als Instrumente der psychologischen Diagnostik. Ein Handbuch*, Heidelberg 1999.

Normal Is the Difference
Maxims for Successful Integration

by Henning Köhler
translated by Genie Sakaguchi

[Note on vocabulary: Mr. Köhler is making a strong case for a new kind of integration, which is quite radical. I have tried to use the words "integrative" or "differentiated integration" where he speaks of this new kind of tolerance, and "integration" or "integrating" where he refers to the old style of integration.]

In this article the curative educator and well-known author Henning Köhler develops concepts to counter a society that is increasingly marginalizing those who are different or disabled, actually threatening to eliminate them altogether. His radical ideas about tolerance bring him to radical maxims for a differentiated integration. This article is a greatly shortened summary of a lecture given on March 13, 2009, in Leipzig, at the founding of the Initiative Integrative Waldorf School.

We stand at a turning point.

It is an open question as to what direction our society and individual human beings will develop. One can be concerned, having the feeling that it's all heading rapidly downhill, when one sees that, apparently, all human intelligence and creativity are directed exclusively towards the development of new technology, and human beings work towards becoming the creators of a new human being. Tiny chip-driven robots could be placed in the bloodstream to keep watch over the individual's health. Psychotropic drugs and genetic technology could allow for many kinds of manipulation of human beings. One hopes that all illnesses could be eliminated, and human beings could be made immortal.

Others fear that new weapons of destruction will arise that can no longer be contained, and they will be used, nevertheless, to rule. On the other hand, a longing for spiritual life lives in society, especially among young people. Spiritual life is seen to be tied to the great social-ethical questions, including the questions of what to do so that human beings no longer suffer hunger or injustice, and also that those who are different, who deviate from the norm will not be shut out, literally, not be excluded from life, as has already been happening for a long time as a result of prenatal diagnostics.

Spirituality today cannot be imagined without a social ethic capable of meeting and transforming the future. And perhaps both can be connected with new technologies, upon which something like a new age, in the best sense, can begin.

Can we get a grip on everything with psychotropic drugs?

The French philosopher, Michel Foucault (1926–1984), was perhaps the greatest theoretician on power, its structures and its psychological backgrounds. Foucault took up the theme of integration early on, making clear that not only exclusion but also inclusion (the German word *Einschliessung* is ambiguous, as it can mean "internment" or "integration") are both instruments of power. He describes how modern strategies of standardization or normalization, the inner disciplining of human beings approaches forms of absolute power. In this connection he also spoke of the development of a new power that he called "biopower." What he meant by this, to put it briefly, is discipline of the spirit through discipline of the physical body. The power to inflict or threaten social or physical death has become the power to rule and control the lives of human beings. And the means by which human lives are controlled, in part without even being noticed, have become ever more subtle.

It begins with education and training and continues in employment dependent on payment, as well as with consumer pressures, applied through the fashion and entertainment industries and the influence of the media. We are regulated by the government and subjected to standardization through the educational process—an organization of the masses by means of which, expressed in neurobiological terms, the brains of human beings are conditioned to certain thought patterns, basic convictions, and structures of consciousness.

The American cultural critic, Francis Fukuyama, has written a book with the title *The End of History and the Last Man* (2002). He warns about the newest developments in genetic technology and pharmacology. He sees these as the greatest dangers of the present. Fukuyama devotes one chapter to the madness with which so-called hyperactive children are treated. He sees in this an indication of what he calls "social control through psycho-pharmacology." According to his view, there are forces at work that intend to control the population down to the smallest details with available chemical and genetic means, to bring about in this way "social peace," to control everything that appears to be different. Would this be the triumph of biopower?

Normal is that which does not stand out.

The concept of integration is already loaded. It refers to a whole, the members of which play specific, assigned roles in the functioning of the whole. The members are not thought of as individuals at all. A human being who does not fulfill his expected role as a part of the whole is a human being in need of integration. The prototypical case of a society of human beings in which every single person is totally integrated, that is, in which every impulse of individuality is brought to a halt, is the military. The military marching order is an example of complete integration.

What does this mean for the foundation of an integrative school? If we say we have twenty-five children, four of whom are in need of integration, what do we actually mean by this? Do we mean that we have a class of normal children, and then four or five abnormal children are added, who, in the course of two or three years if it's a good integrating school, will likewise become normal? Is that what we want? This is basically the central idea of many integrating institutions until now: normalization. Integrating a few unusual children into a larger group of normal children so that the behavior of these eccentrics is ever more adapted to the norm. Can that be the point?

Normal is the difference.

The ideal thought that one can oppose such a point is the concept of the individual. Every person has the right to be accepted into the community and, indeed, in such a way that his own individuality is not threatened, is not brought into question, but rather, to the contrary, is encouraged and promoted. From this point of view, it seems to me to be appropriate to speak of a differential integration (DI), as opposed to ordinary integration.

DI intends that human beings with obvious differences should be received by others, without the background thought being that these differences should be driven out. DI means giving up the expropriating of an individual's life-destiny through reference to an abstract average standard; it means that the difference of the other person, even when we experience this, to begin with, as something strange, will be affirmed and carried by the community.

Normal is the difference. We welcome variety. We celebrate the differences. In the ideal case we will do all we can to find forms of community-building in schools and in other places in which this great variety is allowed to live. For all the theoretical stress on the individual over the past one hundred years, we certainly have not yet come very far in discovering what tolerance means in reality.

Genuine tolerance is radical.

True tolerance—I would call it radical tolerance, because it actually goes to the root—does not mean to simply tolerate the difference of the other, but rather take joy in it. This is a tolerance that leads us to discover a new field of enthusiasm: Just as you are in your unbelievably interesting and, for me, also at first mysterious, otherness, just so would I want you to be. For me, it is a continual occasion to wake up the otherness of the other person to perceive, to fathom, and to appreciate.

In my view, the true curative teacher would be one for whom the so-called handicap of the so-called handicapped person is a constant source of joyful astonishment, which by no means excludes that he feel compassion when he meets suffering, but that impulse is not reserved for the so-called realm of the so-called handicapped; opportunities for compassion can be found every day and everywhere. It should fill us with enthusiasm that every human being is a universe unto himself—and where can this be better studied than in curative education? That would be an active, radical tolerance that can become a trend-setting, community-building force. Besides, these ideals are also just as true for "normal" teachers and, actually, for all who have to do with education.

More and more ways of behaving are being seen as pathological.

The boundaries for what is considered normal and acceptable have been increasingly narrowed in the last decades. The internationally used lists of psychological disturbances of children and young people have expanded explosively since the middle of the 1980s. There are constantly new syndromes. More and more types of behavior, formerly seen as variations of the norm, are now classified as pathological. For these reasons it is at least an open question whether we actually have more disturbed children than in earlier times.

The increasing categorizing of deviant behaviors as pathological, the swelling of therapeutic programs, the shifting of pedagogical problems over to the realm of medical responsibility—all this does not help us get on top of the situation. Children as they are today do not need ever more therapy and ever more regulation and ever more standards and ever more integration. They need more social warmth. And more attention. These are the decisive factors: warmth and attention. Warm attention. Attention from the heart.

What is not meant here is the supervising, controlling, assessing attention towards which our time tends so strongly. There is another kind of attention that is something very much of the future, but which we can already begin to practice today. Rudolf Steiner describes this attention as a new, purified form of interest in the other person, whose education has put us in the position to see the "divine" in that person.

We should take the trouble to develop the new kind of seeing that brings about an inner transformation with reference to how one looks at children, in particular how one looks at special children, how one can distance oneself from false ideas of standards, and from that "gaze that searches for errors" that we all are more or less conditioned to use.

Maxims for a different kind of integration

In the following I would like to set forth the fundamental maxims for a differentiated integration, that is, an integration that is "free from standards."

1. Dividing people into handicapped and not-handicapped is, first of all, tactless with regards to the supposed handicapped people, and second, it's

an untruth. To be handicapped is such a definitive criterion for being human in general that one can say with certain correctness: A person's humanity really breaks through only when he perceives and accepts in himself his own fundamental handicap. This concerns every one of us. In that moment when I perceive and accept myself in my own handicapped situation, I have an inner insight that forbids me ever again to say to, or to think of, another human being: "In contrast to me, you are handicapped."

2. To be sure, there are varying gifts and talents in specific areas. If one takes all human beings as a totality, the scale from "less gifted" to "average gifted" to "highly gifted" would be unnecessary. Every person is equally highly gifted, but not all are able to reveal their gifts equally well, and not all have the good fortune to gain recognition for their talents.

3. Standardized measurements for intelligence give information, at the most, about a very small portion of the spectrum of intelligence. To certify a person as being of lower intelligence is speculation. Our interest should be directed not at the degree of intelligence a person shows, but rather how and where his intelligence is expressed or why it cannot express itself.

4. To equate normality and good health is neither plausible nor sensible. Normalization is not an ideal of pedagogy, or of curative pedagogy.

5. The monopoly of the neurobiological interpretation in the curative realm cannot be tolerated. It is historically a throwback. Thirty years ago it seemed that the time of believing that all deviant characteristics and behavioral types could be traced to a single cause of defects in the physiology of the brain was finally over. But now the phrenology of the 19th century is making a rousing comeback in newly expressed forms. Besides, we Germans especially should never again fall into the error of viewing so-called handicapped fellow human beings as biologically defective. After Auschwitz, that should be finished once and for all.

6. Within the conceptual framework of differential integration, we will champion certain ideas that have been systematically mocked and discredited in postmodern discourse—ideas such as "I," "soul," spirit" and "destiny." It is a matter of newly characterizing and justifying these ideas in the context of a post-materialistic anthropology capable of working into the future. It is not enough merely to postulate them.

7. Schools, and most especially integrative schools, should be places where children—as Jean Paul once expressed it—would be strengthened to withstand the "illnesses of the times." They should not be places where children are trained to behave as "inconspicuously" as possible. Almost nothing stands in the way of a true curative-pedagogical view as much as "the demand for conformity." (Juerg Jegge)

8. The philosophy of the differentiated integration proceeds from the understanding that every human being enters the world with a biographical impulse or intention. One could also speak of an individual's "guiding will," as Goethe called it. Besides genetics and environment/education, there is a third element [in the development of a child.] This third element should be sacred to us. We are called upon to develop an "appreciating feeling" for this element. (Edmund Husserl) Strong, passionate will impulses of a child must never be fought or shown to be laughable—even when we doubt that it's an expression of that inner guiding will. We could be mistaken. Unswerving, stoical refusals by a child must never be contemptuously passed over. It could have to do with an "inner imperative" whose meaning is still hidden from us.

9. The current practice of blaming parents for the misbehavior and school failures of their children is unproductive and mostly factually inaccurate. Children are not just the products of their education. Parents are partners in a good integrative school—and not just those who come, bowed and heavy with guilt, to enter into an alliance when we are dissatisfied with their child.

10. Respect for the "otherness" of the other is the great learning objective. Rudolf Steiner called the highest form of this respect "awe before destiny." A child must never be humiliated.

11. The lessons, as far as possible, should be arranged in such a way that the different constellations of talents and varieties of intelligence find equal consideration. Each child should experience, at least once a week, his competence, and feel his particular areas of interest addressed. In this regard, the results of recent research into intelligence and talents should be called upon.

12. Bullying among the children will lessen the more the adults make the effort to arrange the life of the school so that a social field of warmth is created. It's a matter of setting the example of social competence. Exhortations fall on deaf ears. The "good" (trust, fairness, helpfulness, and tolerance) must live in the air, to a certain degree, so that the children can "smell" it. They will register, with joy and relief: "Here the people treat each other respectfully, and us, too." Here the teachers and parents speak with each other in such a way that true recognition is perceptible. So, where it has to do with the social climate, let us begin with ourselves. It will pay off!

13. What we think about the children has exactly the same effect as if it were spoken. Our speech, for example in the conferences (child studies), should always be very careful. Then we will notice that our thoughts also gradually become more careful.

14. Every lack or defect that we believe we have seen in a child must be balanced out with at least two good qualities, strengths, beautiful aspects that we have discovered in the child in our contemplative judgment. Then we will have the inner attitude with which the differentiated integration can succeed.

Anything but Children's Play
What Play in School Means for Learning

by Irene Jung
translated by Genie Sakaguchi

A research project at the Rudolf Steiner School in Hamburg-Bergstedt investigates what play in the school means for learning. This is part of a larger research project with the theme "Independent [self-reliant] Learning," conducted under the supervision of the Academy for Developmental Mentoring and supported financially by Software AG-Stiftung. The participating teachers carry out individual projects that they hope will encourage individual work and learning; they evaluate the results and incorporate the results in the lessons. The author of this article conducted the following research project.

It's eight-thirty in the morning, outside in the schoolyard.

The class teacher of Grade Four, Knut Krödel, observes the boys in his class standing by the garden plot next to a side wing of the school building. There are two groups pelting each other with the bark mulch that is scattered in the garden. There is also quite a bit of mulch scattered all over the pavement next to the garden. Immediately the teacher hurries over to the boys. But before he can begin his admonition, one of the boys comes over to him to say: "Everything is all right. We have set up rules. Afterwards we will sweep it all up." And in fact, a half hour later the bark mulch has disappeared from the pavement and is neatly distributed in the garden. For three days the children play this game, and on each day they clean up after the game.

A few weeks later, at the same time, in an abandoned corner behind the gym, the children of the Fourth Grade want to build a climbing structure. To begin they dig out the earth one meter deep in four locations. The first thirty centimeters is pretty easy to dig, but the rest is very difficult work. After that four posts are cemented in place. Then, suddenly, they are no longer interested. The four posts satisfy them. The class teacher encourages them to keeping going with the project, but without success. They are already heading for another corner of the schoolyard.

Shouldn't these children already be in the classroom? What does playing with mulch and building a climbing structure have to do with school?

Whether that is actually school

"And whether that is school," says the class teacher, Knut Krödel. For one whole year, with the children of his Fourth Grade class, he has carried out the project, "Playing before Main Lesson." Every morning, shortly after eight o'clock, after arriving in the classroom, greeting each other and saying the morning verse, they headed outside.

Here the children were allowed to play in the spacious, idyllically laid-out school yard for one whole hour, according to their heart's desire, in the wind and weather, without any direction or instruction from their teacher. He was, to be sure, always present and was the contact person when the children needed help, and he played with them from time to time, when the children invited him, but otherwise he held himself apart and observed. This was all with the permission of the parents. How did it come about?

"After long observation I had perceived that around nine years of age children lose their will to learn, and they experience more problems with learning. Often I heard this sentence: 'School just isn't fun for me any more.' The parents, as well, told me that their children were groaning in the morning, from the time of waking through going to school. How can this be? I thought to myself, 'We want to bring about exactly the opposite!'"

Other considerations connected with these thoughts. What does learning actually mean? Waldorf schools with their holistic approach have never understood learning to be just an accumulation of knowledge or the product of the visible work of the student. This can be seen in the many musical lessons, as well as the many other common social undertakings such as the monthly assemblies, the fairs, the festivals that are put on by the children working together. These things not only build a sense of community and give a glimpse of the actual lessons, but they also foster the perceptual capacities of the students, as well as their creative imagination and their joy in discovery. Along with these aspects, they also encourage, often in a playful way, their entire personality.

Naturally, even in Waldorf schools, the original form of play is displaced by the canon of subjects that must be taught. Play remains something that the child can only give himself up to after his other obligations—schoolwork, homework, often private music or sports lessons, and chores—have all been met.

Often, however, not even then is there any time for play. Since the television, the computer, and electronic games have gained entry into the children's bedrooms, play has increasingly fallen further and further into the background. The potential results for the development of the child's personality, not to mention the effect on the acquisition of necessary academic capacities for learning, are well known. The numbers continue to grow, of students who are not able to concentrate on their work for more than a few minutes in a lesson, who cannot work alone, and who cannot complete a task once it is begun, or only with great difficulty. It was to counter these developments that the "Play hour" was instituted at the Rudolf Steiner School in Hamburg-Bergstedt. Class teacher Knut Krödel resisted the usual separation between play and instruction.

Children learn during play.

"When do children learn? Children learn while they are playing! To begin with, they learn about the outer things of the world. They must come to know that the things with which they are surrounded can be changed by their activity. They can have an influence on the world. Children often have different ideas about the changes they would like to make, and then in the actual doing, they learn how things really stand.

"In every game there are rules that are invented. The children test the rules and themselves, in so far as they pay attention to the reactions of their peers and their environment. In this process they learn a great deal. I have observed that children always set up rules in their play together. And consequences are immediately applied when there is a violation. In this way children learn to be fair. The one who always wants to be the leader will soon realize that his playmates turn away from him. So they must find compromises, in order for the game to continue. It is fascinating to watch children in this process. In this way they are learning social competence. In contrast, no child learns social competence when the teacher tells him how he should behave."

Awakening the joy of learning

To re-enliven and stimulate the children's joy in learning was the great goal that Knut Krödel hoped to bring about with his project. A further objective was to find an answer to the tantalizing questions: What kind of impact would play have on the one and a half hour main lesson that followed immediately after the play hour? Would the children retain the trust in their own capacities and their own initiative? Would they be more curious, more imaginative, have more joy in discovering things? How did the social relations develop among the children?

In answer to these questions, the class teacher replied: "All the students came into the lesson with high spirits and an even temper, they worked joyfully, and had no difficulties joining in with the lesson and following along. At the same time they were able to achieve much more than the previous two fourth grade classes that I had taught in earlier class cycles. They learned fractions, for example, in a shorter, more intense period of time, with greater certainty. I also noticed a great difference in writing dictation between this group of students and earlier fourth grades. And they began to help one another more, which I also attributed to the play period."

The children begin to learn on their own.

In the fifth grade, during the 2009–10 school year, the play hour was changed. The time allowed to play outside became a free hour "at [the child's] disposal." This was to take into account the age of the children, now heading into prepuberty. In addition they investigated in which direction the period would develop under the new conditions. This showed that the children were learning to manage their own time. Often they went outside to play, and then at other times they played in the classroom. But they no longer only played.

On many days, as a matter of course, they worked at their desks in their main lesson books, or quizzed each other on their vocabulary words, gave each other dictation to write, or practiced for a report. Once in a while the class teacher was asked for help, for example when a child had not understood a new lesson. This independence was also observed by the teacher in the main lessons that followed: "The children have slowly gained in form, and it seems that the play time has borne fruit. It seems that what they learned there has worked on in other subjects. When I teach them French, they learn eagerly and with joy. In the main lesson block about Egypt, I notice that they show tremendous joy and curiosity in their reports. Almost every day we experience that a child has come up with a new, creative idea to make everything interesting. It all started with a talk by K., who spoke about the pyramids. She brought in a pyramid that she had made herself, and after her talk she even gave a quiz to the students, to see if they had been paying attention.

"Today E. and P. came in and spoke about Ramses. They had large beautiful pictures and even some photos, too. As the main attraction—they had wrapped up a child, to show what happened to the excavator when he unwrapped the mummy. T. had made a little ship out of papyrus. But it was J. who took the cake, as he spoke about chariots, and presented a large drawing on the blackboard, that was appreciated by all with a great 'Ah.'"

And what did the students have to say [about this project]? In a written survey at the end of the fifth grade, of the 38 children who participated, 24 said that since the project began, they were much happier to come to school, and 19 children said that they could learn much better since the beginning of the project. 23 children said they would like to keep the play hour in the coming school year. And only 12 children wrote that the play hour was not so important.

Now an interesting task begins for the class teacher to pursue: to find out what kind of lasting effects the playtime during the past two years will have on the present learning of the children.

Love Enables Knowledge

by Lorenzo Ravagli
translated by Genie Sakaguchi

Two ideas—or should we rather say, world powers?—revolve around the biography of Rudolf Steiner: Knowledge and Freedom. Knowledge is based on and culminates in Freedom. The source and completion of Freedom is Love.

> *The rainbow mirrors human love and strife;*
> *Consider it and you will know:*
> *In many-hued reflection we have life.*
> Goethe, *Faust*, Part II

For Steiner, knowledge always had a mystical, religious dimension: Its implementation is, first and last, Theophany. "Becoming aware of the idea in reality is the true communion of Mankind." (CW 1, *Goethe: Natural-Scientific Writings*, 1887) "The life filled with thought content in reality is at the same time a life with God." (CW 4, *The Philosophy of Freedom*, 1893) "Anthroposophy is a path of knowledge that would like to lead the spiritual in the human being to the spiritual in the cosmos." (CW 26, *Anthroposophic Guiding Principles*, 1924)

The essence of freedom is love, devotion, and humility—they also point beyond the isolated existence of this world and bring a person closer to something that is greater than himself. "Not insofar as a human being investigates some laws of God is he acting according to the intentions of God, but rather insofar as he acts according to his own insights. For in [his own insights] live the intentions of God." (CW 2, *Outlines of an Epistemology of the Goethean Worldview*, 1886) "Only an action arising out of love can be a moral one. … Only the person who acts out of love for the deed, who directs his devotion to objectivity, is truly free in his actions." (CW 1, 1887) "The event of Golgotha is a free cosmic deed of love within the history of the earth; it can only be grasped by the love that a human being can summon to this comprehension." (CW 26, 1924)

Whoever takes a look at the public life of Rudolf Steiner will be able to see easily that the driving force in the first half of his life (from 1883 to 1904) was the idea of Knowledge, and that the second half (1904–1925) was dominated by the idea of Love. The two halves of his life, each of 21 years, mirror each other on a vertical axis that lies in the year 1904. This is the axis around which, in the life of Rudolf Steiner, the eternal broke through into the temporal, and the temporal stood before the countenance of the eternal, the eternally-present: "The evolution of my soul rested upon the fact that I stood before the Mystery of Golgotha in most inward, earnest joy of knowledge."[1] (CW 28, *The Story of My Life*, 1923)

In the light of this remarkable fact, one could speak of two streams: One comes out of the past, hastening towards the future, while the other flows out of the future and strives towards the past. The stream out of the past is the stream of knowledge, through which the human being lives more and more into the foundation of the world. The stream from the future is the stream of love, through which the human being more and more grows out of the foundation of the world. This observation calls to mind the memory of an aphorism of Walter Benjamin's on a picture by Paul Klee, titled *Angelus Novus*: "It shows an angel who seems about to move away from something he stares at. ... This is how the angel of history must look. His face is turned toward the past. Where a chain of events appears before us, he sees one single catastrophe, which keeps piling wreckage upon wreckage and hurls it at his feet. The angel would like to stay, awaken the dead, and make whole what has been smashed. But a storm is blowing from Paradise and has got caught in his wings; it is so strong that the angel can no longer close them. This storm drives him irresistibly into the future to which his back is turned. ... What we call progress is this storm."[2]

But we could also see the angel of history in another way. Paradise lies not in the past, but in the future, and the storm is not driving the angel, but rather pulling him. What is pulling him is the love that is working out of the future. And the angel is not moving through time, but rather, time moves through the angel, while he stands in the eternal present with a backwards glance. The great secret of human existence that makes it all possible is now: How does knowledge become love and constantly renew itself out of love? We could also formulate it so: How does "the science of freedom" become "the reality of freedom"?

The two indicated aspects are found in the life of every human being; they are just a bit more clearly pronounced in Steiner's life because his life as a whole had something of a paradigmatic character. They are actually to be found in every wakeful moment of life, for knowledge always goes over into action, and action into knowledge. We do not change the world through our knowledge. Through our actions, on the other hand, we do change the world: We would not act if we did not want to change it.

To the truly seeing-eye of the angel, the context of the world appears not only as a succession of disasters, but also, at the same time, as order, full of wisdom, a cloth woven of hidden harmonies. The closer our knowledge comes to the ground of being, out of which all relationships emerge, the more this knowledge is transformed, along with its subject and the one who knows. What first appears to us as lawfulness, turns out, in its depths, to be formative will that shows this lawfulness.

The laws of nature, according to Steiner, are in reality, living relationships among beings of the hierarchies. And the more that the seeing-eye adapts to this formative will of the world, all the more will it be gripped and moved by it. Wisdom will become love, and this love comes from out of the future to meet him. Love that embraces the past and the future makes it possible for us to act out of knowledge.

NOTES
1. Translation of quote from Rudolf Steiner's biography was taken from: http://wn.rsarchive.org/Books/GA028/TSoML/GA028_c26.html;mark=210,38,57#WN_markFeb. 7, 2012.
2. Translation of Walter Benjamin quote taken from: http://epc.buffalo.edu/authors/bernstein/shadowtime/wb-thesis.html, Feb. 7, 2012.

Methods before Age Nine

by Ted Warren

Introduction

In the lectures Rudolf Steiner held on education, we find a peculiar combination of four major topics:

1. *Educational principles which give our work direction,*
2. *Methods for how we can teach and how children can learn,*
3. *Knowledge of the human being that helps us understand how our children develop, and*
4. *Exercises for teachers that can help us develop the right mood for our work.*

None of these topics is given in isolation, and together they create a vast resource that teachers, parents and children can develop further during the coming centuries.

Between 1919 and 1924 Rudolf Steiner expanded on these topics in roughly two hundred lectures. All four sources of educational insight and practice are given according to the child's ideal development in the stages of: before the age of nine, before the age of twelve, before the age of fourteen and after the age of fourteen. This essay covers the first stage of Waldorf education, before children reach their ninth year, as Rudolf Steiner introduced these opportunities to the new and inexperienced teachers at the first Waldorf school in late August 1919. The course is known as *Practical Advice to Teachers*.

Educational principles

During these initial fourteen lectures, Rudolf Steiner developed eleven guiding principles for work with children before the age of nine. These principles are intimately connected to the methods he suggested as well as the knowledge of the human being he developed. I take them out of their context in those lectures to highlight them here.

At the Waldorf school we do not simply use artistic activities to educate our children, the entire learning process comes from the artistic realm. Why is this so? The artistic element works particularly strongly on the will nature of children. The activities enable the children to penetrate into something that is connected with their whole being, not merely something that takes place in their head. This strengthens their interest in the entire world. No matter what subject we teach, the artistic element permeates the lessons, even in conventional activities such as writing and reading and arithmetic. Soul substance, or more vividly expressed, nutrition for the soul of the child is taught each day. The key to Waldorf education in the early years is to help the children combine meaningful movements with inner picture creativity each day.

In the very first lessons in the first grade, every child learns to draw and paint-draw. Then we foster music so they can handle a musical instrument. Artistic feeling is awakened and the children sense something in their entire being that is more than the conventional learning process.

Steiner's educational principles not only provide direction for the teachers educational development but also for the school's organization. We work together on the principles. In these introductory lectures I have found eleven principles that cover such powerful themes as: harmonizing the spirit and soul human being with the bodily nature, allowing the children to experience the inner law of things they experience in the world, using antipathy to comprehend and sympathy to love, and striving to balance out the polarities in the children by using two streams of art, the sculptural/ pictorial forces with the musical/ poetical forces.

Further principles challenge teachers to use their courage to invent their own examples of content in the lessons and present them enthusiastically. Teachers of arithmetic should proceed from the whole to the parts, so the child is thereby placed in the world in a living way. Teachers should not drill children to respect authority but act in a way that will help the children's feeling for authority arise. We should educate the children's will, not by forcing them to use their will to understand the meaning of everything, but by letting them do things that do not require them to lay bare the meaning of things: by introducing rhythm, beat, melody, the harmony of colors, repetition, and many other activities including playing!

We nourish the children's heart forces and inner life of feeling when they learn something by heart without understanding it and without explanations of the meaning, if they remembers at a later date what they have learned and now understand it more fully. Lastly, we guide the children into drawing and painting and into the music realm to develop their will, which supports them when they move from gymnastics into eurythmy. Below you can read Rudolf Steiner's own words and you will discover new dimensions to these principles.

Educational Principle #1

Our method will deal with the harmonizing of the higher man, the man of spirit and soul, with the physical, bodily nature, the lower man. The subjects you teach will not be treated in the way they have been dealt with hitherto. You will have to use them as means with which to develop the soul and bodily forces of the individual in the right way. What matters for you will not be the transmitting of knowledge as such; you will be concerned with handling the knowledge for the purpose of developing human capacities. You will have to distinguish between subject matter which rests on convention or tradition and knowledge founded on a recognition of universal human nature.[1]

Educational Principle #2

What should live within the children is their inner closeness to the forms themselves, be they in nature or on the blackboard. Between the ages of seven and fourteen we strive to awaken a sense for the inner law of things. This does not happen by mere copying. The sense for the inner law of things will enable the individual to cope with life later on.[2]

Educational Principle #3

For the child's life of will you will be a good educator if you endeavor to surround every individual with sympathy, with real sympathy. These things also belong to education: antipathy that enables us to comprehend and sympathy that enables us to love.[3]

Educational Principle #4

As educators we shall have the task of constantly quickening what is dead and protecting what is approaching death in the human being from dying entirely; indeed, we shall have to fructify this dying with the quickening element we develop out of the will. Therefore we must not be apprehensive about starting right from the beginning with a certain artistic form in our lessons while the children are still young.

Now everything artistic that comes towards mankind is divided into two streams: the sculptural, pictorial stream and the musical, poetical stream. These two streams of art—the sculptural and pictorial and the musical and poetic—are indeed polar opposites, though just because of their polarity they are also especially capable of a higher synthesis, a higher union.[4]

Educational Principle #5

Ask yourself, what is more important? To take in a historical fact with great effort and then strenuously weave it into your lessons, or to invent your own examples to offer to your pupils with your own enthusiasm?[5]

Educational Principle #6

Just as in arithmetic we start not from the addenda but from the sum which we divide into parts, so here too we proceed from the whole to the parts. The advantage is to place the child in the whole world in a living way. The child maintains permanent links with the living whole if we proceed this way. Learning individual letters from pictures gives the child a link to the living reality.[6]

Educational Principle #7

We do not drill children to respect authority, but by acting in a way that will help their feeling for authority to arise, for instance by teaching spelling in a way that places it on a foundation of authority.[7]

Educational Principle #8

If you want to do the best you can for an individual's faculty of cognizing through thought, you will have to analyze the meaning of everything that he is to take in and retain. It is indeed a fact that by first one-sidedly analyzing the meaning of everything we can go a long way in the education of man's observation of the world. But we would go nowhere in educating his will, for we cannot force the will to emerge by throwing a strong light on the meaning of anything. The will wants to sleep, it does not want to be awakened fully by what I might call the perpetual unchaste laying bare of meaning.

Human life calls for more than education in the realm of meaning, it calls for education in what the will experiences in its sleeping condition: rhythm, beat, melody, the harmony of colors, repetition, any kind of activity not calling for a grasp of meaning.[8]

Educational Principle #9

For thinking and knowing we must certainly undertake measures that involve the revelation of meaning: reading, writing and so on. For willed activity we must cultivate everything that does not involve just the interpretation of meaning but requires to be directly grasped by the whole human being: everything artistic. What lies between these two will work mainly on the development of the feeling life, of the heart forces. These heart forces are strongly affected if the child is given the opportunity of first learning something by heart without understanding it and without explanations of the meaning, though of course there is a meaning, and if he then later, when he is matured through other processes, remembers what he has learned and now understands what he took into him. This subtle process must be taken into account in teaching if we want to bring up human beings who have an inward life of feeling.[9]

Educational Principle #10

All these things, painting-drawing and drawing-painting, and also the finding of their way into the music realm will be, for us, during the children's first year at a school, a wonderful element in developing their will, which is something almost totally removed from present-day schools. And if we can also lead over ordinary gymnastics into eurythmy, we shall be promoting their will development to a special degree.[10]

These educational principles given by Rudolf Steiner have been used by teachers and schools during the past ninety-three years. In addition teachers have created their own principles and schools have worked together on their principles. Steiner gave us direction, he did not create dogmas that anyone should follow. No one has the answer to education. We can continually renew our work according to what we see in our children.

Methods

For our work with children before the age of nine, Steiner gave to the original teachers during the first lectures not only principles, but approximately thirty-six methods. After twenty-one years of teaching I was led to these lectures one evening by some tough questions:

- How many methods do I use in the course of a main lesson?
- How much time do I spend preparing content and how much time do I spend preparing methods?
- Which methods do I use in the subject lessons?
- What are my methods in the social interaction in the class?

I also realized there are two sides to these questions:

- Which methods do all of my children need during the main lessons?
- Which methods of learning do my children use in order to learn when I teach?
- Which methods do they need in the subject lessons?
- And in their social interaction, which methods do my children use each day?

These questions led to new questions. I searched for a better understanding of my pupils' learning styles. In the parent conferences that semester in Princeton I asked the parents to tell me how their children learn. We compared notes and a picture of the peculiar needs arose. I also realized the learning style of each child lies deep within his or her soul and it will continue throughout high school, college and their professional lives. Therefore I decided to restudy the introductory lectures by Steiner to see how he prepared the first teachers, particularly with methods.

The Waldorf school movement has grown and prospered for close to a century, yet it feels like we have only just begun in terms of using the original *methods* taught by Rudolf Steiner. And we have only just begun to develop our own methods based on the *educational principles* and our *knowledge of the human being*. The real questions I face every day is: How do I teach my pupils and how do they need to learn? When we look into their eyes and read their faces, they show us more than words can describe. My job is to respond to those perceptions.

Let us deepen our understanding of the methods Steiner introduced for children before the age of nine within the following categories:

- The first day of school
- The next lessons
- Painting
- Drawing
- Music
- Eurythmy
- The role of feeling and the will
- Writing and reading
- Arithmetic
- Vowels and consonants
- Grammar
- Spelling
- Penmanship
- Storytelling
- Nature

The first day of school

Certainly one of the biggest experiences in any Waldorf teacher's career is the first lesson on the first day of school. You present something that will continue to enliven all of the following lessons. And all of the following lessons will be used to make that which takes in the first lesson more and more valuable for the child's entire education.

Steiner spoke to his teachers as if he were holding the first lesson. All of the children are in the classroom for the first time and he tells them: "You have now come to school. Now I will tell you why you have come to school. You have come to school to learn something. As yet, you have no idea of all the things you will be learning in school, but there will be all sorts of things that you will have to learn. Why will you have to learn all sorts of things in school? Well, you have no doubt met some adults and you must have noticed that they can do something that you cannot do. And so that one day you will be able to do what the grown-ups can do is the reason why you are here. One day you will be able to do something that you cannot do yet.

"Look how grown-ups have books and can read. You can't read yet. But you will learn to read and when you have learned how to do it, you will also be able to take the books and learn from them what the grown-ups can learn from them. Grown-ups can write letters to each other; in fact they can write down anything they like. Later on you will also be able to write letters, for as well as learning to read, you will also learn to write. As well as reading and writing, grown-ups can also do sums. You don't know what doing sums means. But you have to be able to do sums when you go out into life, for instance if you want to buy something to eat or to wear, or if you want to make something to wear. You will also learn to do sums."

Then the teacher moves on to something else: "Children, look at yourselves. You have two hands, a left one and a right one. These hands are for working; you can do all kinds of things with them." After you have spoken with the children about their hands, let them do something skillful with their hands. You might even do this in the first lesson. You might say to them:

"Watch me do this. (Draw a straight line.) Now take your hand and do it too!" We let them do this as slowly as possible. It will be a slow process if we let them come to the blackboard one by one, letting them make their mark on the board and then return to their seats. The most important thing is that the children digest the lesson properly. Then you might say:

"Now I am going to do this. (Draw a curved line.) And now you can take your hands and do it too." Each child does so in the air, on the board or both. When they have all finished you say: "This one is a straight line, and this one is a curved line; with your hands you have just made a straight line and a curved line." The teacher should help the clumsier children and each child should do it as accurately as possible from the start.[11]

The next lessons

Let the children make a straight line and a curved line in the following lessons. Steiner suggested you make a straight line on the board again and let the children copy it. Do the same with the curved line. Then you ask individual children: "What is it?" "A straight line!" Then you draw a curved line again and ask them: "What is it?" "A curved line!" The teacher uses the principle of repetition. You let the children copy the drawing and then, let them name it themselves. This is a subtle but very important nuance.

Painting

The first steps in drawing are followed up by the introduction to painting. It is a good idea to take out a box of paints and set aside a glass of water quite soon with the children. After you have pinned a white paper to the blackboard, you take up a brush, dip it in the water, take some paint and make a small yellow patch on the white surface. Then you let each child come forward and paint a similar small patch. Each patch must be separate from the other patches so that in the end you have so and so many yellow patches.

Then you dip the brush in the blue paint and put some blue next to your yellow patch. And then you let the children come forward and put some blue next to the yellow. When about half of them have done that you say: "Now we shall do something else; I am going to dip my brush in the green paint and put green next to the other yellow patches." Avoiding as well as you can making them jealous of each other, you then let the remaining children put on the green in the same way. All this will take a while. It is indeed essential to proceed very slowly, taking only very few small steps in the lesson. The children will digest it well.

Now the time has come for you to say: "I am going to tell you something that you will not yet understand very well, but one day you will understand it very well. What we did at the top, where we put blue next to the yellow, is more beautiful than what we did at the bottom, where we put green next to the yellow!"

This will sink deep into the child's soul. It will be necessary to repeat it several times but he will also ponder it. He will not be entirely indifferent to it. From simple, naïve examples the child will learn to understand how to feel the difference between something beautiful and something less beautiful.[12]

We should introduce the child to colors as early as possible. And it is good to let the child use colors on colored as well as white surfaces. And we should endeavor to awaken in the child the kind of feelings that can arise only out of a spiritual scientific view of the world. One discovers, for instance, when using blue, that it lies within the blue color itself to characterize the whole realm of inward absorption. So if we want to paint an angel moved by inwardness, we quite automatically have the urge to use blue because the nuances of blue, the light and dark blue call forth in the soul a feeling of movement arising out of the soul element.[13]

Drawing

When we guide children into the realm of what can be modeled, we must see to it that they follow the plastic forms with their hands. By feeling the way he makes his own forms, by moving his hand and making a drawing, the child can be brought to follow the forms with his eyes but also with his will emerging through his eyes. It is no violation of the child's naïvete if we teach him to follow the forms of the body with the hollow of his hand or if we make him aware of his eyes, for instance by letting him follow a complete circle with his eyes and then saying: "You are making a circle with your eyes." This does not wound the child's naïvete; it engages the interest of the whole human being. We must therefore be aware that we lift the lower part of the human being up into the higher part, the nerve-sense being.[14]

Music

A similar method may be used when you introduce music into the lesson. It is good to start with one note or another. There is no need to tell the children the name of the note. You simply strike the note in some way. It is good to let the children also strike the note, thus here too combining the lesson with the will element. Afterwards you strike a second, concordant note and then let a number of children strike it too. The next step is to strike a note followed by a discordant note and again let the children do the same. You try, just as before with the colors, to awaken in the children a feeling for concordance and discordance of notes, not by talking to them about concordance and discordance but by speaking of beautiful and less beautiful, thus appealing here also to their feelings. These things and not the letters of the alphabet are the starting points for the early lessons.

The class teacher will hold these conversations with the children. It would be good if the music teacher could conduct similar conversations, though oriented more towards the musical, and go over the same ground again and again. This should help give the school a more cooperative character. In weekly meetings the teachers should develop a cooperation by discussing themes and activities that can bring about unity in the lessons.[15]

In the first year we will not only have singing but also start learning about music in an elementary way with the help of instruments. We should lead them to an instrument in addition to singing. We teach them the first elements of listening to the relationship between notes. And we endeavor to hold the balance between bringing out the musical element from within through song, and listening to the tonal element from outside or the producing of notes through an instrument.[16]

The educational influence we exert by using the musical element must consist in a constant harmonizing by the Apollonian element of the Dionysian element welling up out of man's nature. While it is a deadening influence that has to be quickened by the sculptural, pictorial element, something that is alive in the highest degree in the musical element has to be dampened down so that in music it does not affect the human being too strongly. This is the feeling with which we ought to bring music to the children.

The children should gain a clear idea of elementary music, of harmonies, melodies and so on through the application of elementary facts, through the analyzing by ear of melodies and harmonies, so that with music we build up the whole artistic realm in the same elementary way as we do the sculptural, pictorial realm where we similarly work up from the details.

Human beings are brought together as one through music and poetry; they become individuals through sculpture and painting. The individuality is supported more by the sculptural, pictorial element, and society more by the living and weaving in community through music and poetry. Early on the child should know what is truly poetical. It is important to draw the child's attention to the musical element on which each poem is founded. The lesson should be arranged in a way that allows the element of recitation in the school to come as close as possible to the musical element. The abstract explanation of poetry, verging almost on grammatical dissection, spells death of everything that ought to work on the child. The interpreting of poems is something quite appalling.[17]

If we were to use art in its two streams in this way to harmonize the human nature through and through, we should indeed achieve a tremendous amount. Consider alone the fact that something infinitely important in man's harmony with the world is achieved when he sings. Singing is a way of reproducing what is already present in the world. When the human being sings he expresses the momentous wisdom out of which the world is built. We must also not forget that in singing man links the cosmic element of the actual sequence of notes with the human word. This brings something unnatural into singing. We can feel this even in the incompatibility of the sound of poem with its content. It would be a step in the right direction if we could present each line in recitative form and quicken only the rhyming word with melody, so that the line flows along in recitative and the rhyming word is sung in an aria. This would ensure a clear distinction between the sounding of a poem and the words which actually disturb the musical part of man.[18]

Eurythmy

As teachers we bestow upon our children the ability to take their place artistically in workings of the world. A child is a born musician. This inner capacity is most present in the third and fourth years. We should dance with children. Permeating their bodies with elementary eurythmy overcomes heaviness in their limbs. Parents can learn these elements and do eurythmy with their children. Then, at the change of teeth the musical element would remain.

It is from this musical element that the separate senses arise: the musically attuned ear and the eye for shapes and forms. The musically attuned ear and the eye appreciative of line and form are specializations of the total human being. Thus we definitely cherish the idea that in drawing on the artistic element we assimilate into the upper man, the nerve-sense man, the disposition of the entire being. By means of music or by means of drawing or modeling, we lift the realm of feeling up into the intellectual sphere. This must happen in the right way.[19]

It is very important for the school to add another factor to healing the physical body in gymnastics, the physiology of bodily functions, namely healing the soul. A hygiene of the soul is possible when the gym lessons alternate with eurythmy lessons. Eurythmy gives the soul what gymnastics give the physical body. These activities work into each other. We need to educate our children to show respect for their fellow man in the outer world.[20]

The roles of feeling and the will

As regards method, it will have had an extraordinary good effect on the children to have spoken to them so early as the first lessons about writing, reading and arithmetic and how they cannot do these things yet but will learn them all in school. As a result of this, a hope, a wish, a resolve forms in the child and through what you yourself do, he finds his way into the world of feeling through the teacher. This acts as incentive to the realm of the will. This is an educational method: You do not present the children directly with what you want to teach them; instead you leave them for a while in a state of expectation. This has an extraordinarily good effect on the development of the will in the growing human being.[21]

Whatever the circumstances, the education of the heart forces suffers if the children have a new teacher each year who cannot follow up what has been instilled into their souls in previous years. It is a part of the teaching method that the teacher moves up through the school with his pupils. Only if this is done can he work with the rhythms of life.[22]

It is good to consider how quite specific educational motives can be repeated year by year. Select things you want to take with the children, make a note of them and return to something similar every year. This is effective even with abstract subjects. For example, teach addition in the first grade, repeat it in the second grade and teach again in the third grade but in progressive repetitions.[23]

Structure your lessons meaningfully so that you can immediately reveal whatever meaning is contained in all that you have to offer. We can only guess what this demand actually means when we have gradually developed a feeling for life.[24]

If you let the child repeat sentences that he is nowhere near to understanding because he is too young, if you make him learn these sentences by heart, you are not working on his faculty of understanding since you cannot explain the meaning which will only emerge later on for him, but you are working on his will, and that is what you should, indeed must do. You must endeavor to bring to the child things that have an abstract meaning in such a way that, though he cannot understand the meaning as yet, he will be able to do so later on when he is more mature because he has taken them in through repetition and can remember them. If you have done this you have worked on his will. And quite especially you have also worked on his feeling life, and that is something you should not forget.[25]

We have speech to thank for much that lives in our feeling of Self, in our feeling of being a personality. Our feelings can rise to a mood of prayer: I hear speech in the language surrounding me; there the power of the Self flows into me through speech. When you feel this you can awaken the same feeling in the children. Then the feeling of Self will not be awakened to egotism but in other ways. There are two ways to awaken the feeling of Self in children. The false way awakens their egotism, the correct way awakens their will power.[26]

Writing and reading

Waldorf teachers move from the whole to the specific. From drawing we move to writing, from writing to reading handwriting and from reading handwriting to reading print. In this way we build reading skills on the basis of drawing. The child has an inner experience; for example, he sees how a sound he breathes finds its expression in reading and writing.

When the children have reached the point where they can master straight and curved lines with their little hands, show them that there are such things as letters. You may start with the fish and F. The sequence you follow is immaterial and you do not need to proceed in alphabetical order.

Let us see what success we have in proceeding to evolve writing and reading out of your own free imagination. I would now say to the children: "You know what a bath is." (It is very important to have something up your sleeve that can contribute to the children's education. In this sense it is good to use the word 'bath' for it reminds them of cleanliness without admonishing them. Choose examples that help the children think of moral and aesthetic attitudes.) Then continue: You see, when grown-ups want to write down what a bath is they do it like this: *bath*. This is the picture of what you express when you say *bath*, when you mean a bath. Now I let a number of children copy this on the board, just copy it so that whenever they are given something like this it also goes straight into their hands so they take it in not just by looking but with their whole being. Then I say: "Watch how you start to say *bath*; let us look at the beginning of *bath*: B." The children have to be led from saying the whole word *bath* to just breathing the initial sound, as I illustrated with the fish.

The next thing to make clear to them is that just as *bath* is the sign for the whole bath, so B is the sign for the beginning of the world *bath*. Then I explain that a beginning like this can be found in other words. I say: If you say *band* you also start like this; if you say *bow*, like the bow some people wear in their hair, you again start in the same way. Have you ever seen a bear in the zoo? When you start to say *bear* you again breath the same sound. All those words start with the same sound. Thus I lead the child from the whole word to the beginning of the word, finding the transition to the single sound or letter, always finding the initial letter from the whole word.[27]

It is important that you yourselves develop the initial letter in a meaningful way out of the drawing element. You will imagine this very well if you simply use your imagination and say to yourself: The people who first saw such animals as those that begin with B, like beavers and bears, they drew the animal's back, its hind paws standing on the ground and its forepaws lifted up; they drew an animal in the act of rising on to its hind legs, and their drawing turned into a B.

You will always find that the initial letter of a word is a drawing, an animal or plant form or some external object; you can give your imagination free reign and there is no need to delve into cultural histories, which are anyway incomplete. Historically the fact is that if you go back to the most ancient forms of Egyptian writing, which was still a sign-writing, you find a great many copies of objects and animals in the letters. Not until the transition from the Egyptian to the Phoenician culture did the change take place that brought with it the development of the picture into a sign representing a sound. It is this transition that the children must experience over again. Let us therefore gain a clear idea of it ourselves in theory.

When writing first began to develop in ancient Egypt every detail that was written down was written in picture-writing; it was drawn, although the drawing had to be as simplified as possible. If somebody employed in copying this picture-writing made a mistake, if for instance a holy word was misrepresented by him, the scribe was condemned to death. We see how seriously anything connected with writing was taken in ancient Egypt. All writing at that time (3200 BC) consisted of pictures of the kind described. The cultural life was taken up by the Phoenicians who lived more firmly in the external world (2750 BC). By them the initial picture of a word was retained and transferred to represent the sound.

Since we are not here to study Egyptian languages, let me give you an example that is also valid for Egyptians and is most easily adapted in our own language. The Egyptians knew that the sound M could be depicted by watching mainly the upper lip. From this sign the letter emerged that we use for the beginning of the word for mouth, the letter that is also valid for any other word beginning with this sound. In this way the picture-sign for a word became the sign for a sound because the picture for the beginning of the word was used.[28]

We do not build reading and writing exclusively on this method. We remain in the artistic element and use the principle involved here to introduce the letters and then whole sentences. In these sentences the child will notice shapes, for instance the F he has become familiar with in *fish*. He will notice other shapes besides, which through lack of time cannot be dealt with individually. The next step will be to write the different printed letters on the blackboard. And then one day we put a whole long sentence on the board and say to the child: "This is what grown-up people have in front of them when they have formed out everything in the way we formed out the F in *fish*," and so on. Then we teach the child to copy down the writing. We make sure that what he sees passes over into his hands so that he not only reads with his eyes but also forms what he reads with his hands. In this way he will know that he can himself form whatever may be on the blackboard.[29]

After this we may reverse the procedure. We split up the sentence we have written down and by atomizing the words we show the forms of the other letters we have not yet derived from the elements; we proceed from the whole to the parts. For example: horse. The children copy it from the board and then the teacher asks them to write h o r s e. The sequence of starting with the whole and moving to the parts is practiced in everything we teach.

Arithmetic

We use this principle of starting from the whole and proceeding to the parts in everything we teach. We might take a piece of paper and cut it into a number of pieces. Then we count the pieces; let us say there are 24. We say to the children: "Look, I describe these pieces of paper I have cut by what I have written down here, 24 pieces of paper. (It could just have well have been beans.)

"Now watch carefully. I take some of the pieces of paper away and make another little heap with them; then I make a third and a fourth heap. I have made four little heaps out of the 24 pieces of paper. Now I shall count the pieces; you cannot do that yet, but I can. The pieces in the first heap I shall call 'nine,' those

in the second, 'five,' those in the third 'seven,' and those in the fourth 'three.' You see: First I had one single heap, 24 pieces of paper. Now I have four heaps, 9 and 5 and 7 and 3 pieces of paper. It is all the same paper. If I have it all together I call it 24; and if I have it in four little heaps I call it 9, 5, 7 and 3 pieces together." In this way I have taught the child to add up. I did not start with the separate addenda from which a sum total could be derived. This would be quite out of keeping with man's original nature.[30]

Apply the opposite process in order to the next step in arithmetic. You say: "Now I shall put all the pieces of paper together again. Then I shall take some away, making two heaps. And I call the heap I have taken away 'three.' How have I come by this 3? By taking it away from the others. When they were together I called it 24; now I have taken 3 away and call the remainder 21." In this way you proceed to the concept of subtraction.[31]

Vowels and consonants

In order to establish inner contact with the children, we let letters arise from pictures. We always explain the consonants in relation to external objects. Then we do the opposite with vowels, for they express internal feelings, that live in the sympathy we have towards things. For even if we are afraid of something, this fear is founded on some mysterious sympathy. We would not be afraid of something if we did not have a hidden sympathy for it. It is relatively easy to observe that the 'O' sound has something to do with astonishment, the 'U' sound with fear and anxiety, the 'A' sound with admiration and wonder, the 'E' sound with offering resistance, the 'I' sound with drawing near to something, and the 'AOU' with veneration.[32]

Therefore speech is a confrontation between antipathy and sympathy. The sympathy lies in the vowels and the antipathy in the consonants. Insofar as speech consists of vowels it encompasses something musical, and insofar as it consists of consonants it bears within itself something like sculpture and painting. In speech we have a genuine synthesis, a true uniting in the human being of the musical with the plastic element.[33] Once again Steiner leads us back to both streams of art. In doing so he deepens our understanding of the role of sympathy that enables us to love and antipathy that enables us to comprehend in education. You may remember this as educational principle #3 in this essay.

Vowels always render man's inner being and his relationship to the outer world. For example, you are teaching the vowel A. Say to them: "Think of the sun that you see in the morning. Can any of you remember what you did when the sun rose this morning?" Perhaps one or other of the children will remember what they did. If none of them remembers, you will have to help them recall. How they must have stood there and how if the sunrise was very beautiful they must have said: *Ah!*

It is a note of feeling that must be struck, the resonance that sounds in the vowel must be called forth from the feeling. Then you must try to say: "When you stood like that and said *Ah!* it was just as if, from your inner being, a beam of sunlight spread out from your mouth. What lives in you when you see the sunrise, comes out of you and streams forth when you say *AH*. But you do not let all of it stream out, you keep some of it back and then it becomes this sign: *A*."

You should try to clothe with a drawing what lies in the breath when a vowel is spoken. In this way you will find drawings that can show you in a picture how the signs for the vowels have come about.[34]

We can always evolve the vowels out of drawing. For example by appealing to the children's feelings you can try to make them imagine themselves in the following situation: "Think what would happen if your brother and sister were to come to you and say something you did not straight away understand. After a while you begin to understand what they mean. Then what do you say?" One of the children may answer or you may have to point out to them that they would say: "*Eeee.*" (In German this is the letter I.) The shape of the sound *Eee* when it is drawn contains a pointing towards whatever has been understood. Indeed it is a rather rough expression of pointing to something. In eurythmy you find it expressed very clearly. So a simple line becomes an 'I ,' a simple line that ought to be fatter at the bottom and thinner at the top, only instead of that we make a line and express the thinner part with a smaller line above it. In this way every vowel can be derived out of the shape of the aspiration, of the breath.[35]

You need not be at all shy of calling to your aid certain ideas that arouse in the feeling life, something that really did live in the process of cultural development. For example, you could say: "Have you ever seen a tall building with a dome on top? But then you have to make the D upside down so it look likes a half moon on its face. But this was awkward, so people upended it and made D. People wanted to make things simpler so out of the D they made a small d." By always pointing out the transition from form to form and never teaching in an abstract way you help the children to progress so that they can find the genuine transition from the form derived from the drawing at first to the shape the letter really has today in handwriting.[36]

Grammar

What is it we do when we raise unconscious speech to the grammar realm, to the knowledge of grammar? We make the transition with our pupils of lifting speech from the unconscious into the conscious realm. Our purpose is not to teach them grammar in a pedantic way but to raise something to consciousness that otherwise takes place unconsciously. Whether consciously or semiconsciously, man does indeed use the world as a trellis up which to climb in a manner that corresponds to what we learn in grammar. Grammar tells us, for instance, that there are nouns. Nouns are names of objects, for objects that are in a sense self-contained in space. That we meet such objects in life is not without significance for this life of ours. All things that can be expressed by nouns awaken our consciousness to our independence as human beings. By learning to name things with nouns, we distinguish ourselves from the world around us. By calling a thing a table or a chair, we are here and the table or chair is there. And we separate ourselves from the table or chair when we name it.

It is quite another matter to describe things as adjectives. When I say: "The stool is blue," I am expressing something with a noun I am dissociated from; but when I describe it with an adjective, I become one with it again. Thus the development of our consciousness takes place in our relationship to things when we address them; we must certainly become conscious of the way we address.

If I use the verb, as in "The man writes," I not only unite myself with the being about whom I have spoken the verb, I also do with him what he is doing in his physical body. I do what he does, my Self does what he does. When I speak a verb, my Self joins in with what the physical body of the other person is doing. I unite my Self with the physical body of the other when I speak a verb. Our listening, especially with verbs, is in reality always a participation. What is so far the most spiritual part of man participates, only it suppresses the activity.

Only in eurythmy is this activity placed in the outer world. In addition to everything else, eurythmy also gives the activity of listening. When one person tells something, the other listens, he performs in his Self what lives physically in the sounds, but he suppresses it. The Self always does eurythmy in participation, and what eurythmy puts before us through the physical body is nothing other than a making visible of listening. So you always do eurythmy when you listen, and when you actually do eurythmy, you are making visible what you leave invisible when you listen. The manifestation of the activity of the listening human being is in fact eurythmy. It is not something arbitrary but rather in reality the revelation of what the listening human being does. People are of course today fearfully slovenly in themselves, so at first when they listen they do some fearfully bad inner eurythmy. By doing it as it should be done, they raise it until it becomes real eurythmy. Through eurythmy people will learn to listen properly, for nowadays they cannot listen properly.[37]

Then you teach the children the concept of activity, a verb: "Sit in your chair. You are a good child. *Good* is an adjective. But now you stand up and walk. You are doing something. That is an activity. The word you need to describe this activity is a verb." Thus we lead the child to the fact and then we make the transition from the fact to the words. In this way we teach the children without doing too much damage what is a noun, an article, an adjective, a verb.

The most difficult is to understand what an article is because the children cannot yet understand the relationship between the article and the noun. We shall have to flounder in abstractions in order to teach the children what an article is. But they have got to learn it. And it is better to flounder in abstractions, since it is anyway something unnatural, than to think up all sorts of artificial ways of making clear to the children the significance and nature of the article, which is anyway impossible.[38]

Spelling

And if we take pains to converse with the children for a long time and let them do plenty of retelling, making an effort ourselves to speak correctly, then we shall at first introduce the matter of right or wrong spelling by making only a few corrections without introducing the two as different aspects of learning to write. In spelling we remain in the realm of speaking as long as possible and only let this merge into actual correct spelling last of all.[39]

In this, a great deal of what could be revealed as our own individuality is rubbed off in what we have to develop for the sake of living together with others. We should feel that this is so, we should be taught to feel that we do such a thing purely for social reasons. Therefore when you begin to orient your writing lessons towards spelling, your starting point must be a quite specific set of feelings. You will again and again have to point out to the children that they should respect and esteem the grown-ups, that they are themselves growing up into a world that is already formed and waiting to receive them, and that therefore they must take notice of what is already there. This is the point of view from which the children must be introduced to things like correct spelling. Spelling lessons must be run parallel with developing their feeling of respect and esteem for what their predecessors have established.

Spelling must not be taught as an abstraction as though it existed as an absolute on the basis of the divine—or shall we say, law; you must develop in the children the feeling. The grown-ups whom we are to respect spell like this, so we ought to follow their example. From this will result a certain variability in spelling, but it will not be excessive; there will be a certain adapting of the growing child to the world of the grown-ups. And we must count on this adapting. It is not our task to create in him the belief: This is right, this is wrong. The only belief we should arouse, thus building on living authority, is: This is the way the grown-ups do it.[40]

Penmanship

During the second year it appears even more predominantly as a separate subject: good penmanship. Since we shall let writing evolve out of painting and drawing, there will be no need for us to draw a distinction between poor penmanship and good penmanship. We shall endeavor not to distinguish between bad writing and good writing and ensure that all our writing lessons are such that the children always write well, so well that they never distinguish between good penmanship and bad penmanship.[41]

Storytelling

The educator must see to it that the whole being of the child is moved. Consider from this point of view the telling of legends and fairy tales: If you have the right feeling for these and are thus able to tell them out of your own mood, you will tell them in a way that enables the children to feel with their whole body something of what is told. You are then really addressing yourself to the astral body of the child. Something rays up from the astral body into the head, which the child ought to feel there. You should sense that you are gripping the whole child and that it is from the feelings and excitement you arouse that an understanding comes to the child of what you are telling.

You may therefore consider it ideal, when you are telling the child legends or fairy tales or while you draw or paint with him, that you do not explain anything or work with concepts but seek to move the child's whole being so that when he leaves you, he only later out of himself reaches an understanding of what you have told. Try therefore to educate the Self and the astral body from below upwards in such a way that the head and heart follow later. Try not to tell the stories in a way that causes them to be reflected in the head and understanding; tell them in a way that evokes a kind of silent thrilled awe—without limits— and also pleasures and sorrows which echo on when the child has left you and only after a while are transformed into understanding and interest. Try to let your influence arise out of your close intimacy with the children. Try not to arouse interest artificially by counting on sensationalism, attempt rather to achieve an inner connection with the children and then let interest arise out of their own being.

Take a simple example: I want to make clear to the child the continued life of the soul after death. I shall only be deceiving myself and never make it clear to him if I merely teach him theories about the subject. No kind of concept can teach a child under the age of fourteen anything about immortality. I can, however, say to him: "See this chrysalis; it is empty. Once there was a butterfly inside, but it has crept out." I can also show him the process when it happens. It is good to demonstrate such metamorphoses to the child. Then I can make the comparison: "Imagine you yourself are a chrysalis like this. Your soul is in you; later it will emerge just as the butterfly emerges from the chrysalis." This is, of course, rather naïvely put. Now you can talk about this for a long time, but if you yourself do not believe that the butterfly is a picture of the human soul, you will not achieve much with the child when you use the comparison. You ought not allow yourself the utter untruth of seeing the whole idea merely as a comparison. It is not just a made-up comparison but a fact placed before us by the divine world order. The two things are not just invented by our intellect. And if out attitude to such things is right, we learn to believe in the fact that nature offers us comparisons for actualities in the realm of soul and spirit.

The child must understand not merely through his ears; communication must be from soul to soul. If you take notice of this you will make progress.[42]

During the first year cultivate as much simple speaking and conversation with the children as possible. We read aloud as little as possible but prepare ourselves so well we can bring to them in a narrative way whatever we want to tell them.

Then we seek to reach the point where the children are able to retell what they have heard from us. We avoid using passages that do not stimulate the imagination and make as much use as possible of passages that stimulate the imagination really strongly, namely fairy tales, as many fairy tales as possible.

And having practiced this telling and retelling with the children for a long time, we then start in a small way to let them give brief accounts of something they have themselves experienced. For instance, we let a child tell us something he likes telling about. With all this telling of stories, retelling, and telling of personal experiences we develop without being pedantic about it the transition from the local dialect to educated speech. This transition is necessary in German-speaking countries and many other countries.[43]

Nature

There is something, that we must not neglect when we take the children out into the mountains or the fields, when we take them out into nature. We must always remember that lessons on natural science have their right place only inside the classroom. Let us assume that we step with the children out into nature where we draw their attention to a stone or a flower. In doing so we should strictly avoid any allusion to what we teach inside the classroom. Out of doors in natural surroundings, we should draw the children's attention to nature in a way that is totally different from the method we use in the classroom. We should never forget to point out to them: We take you out into the open so that you may feel the beauty of nature, and we bring the products of nature into the classroom so that indoors we can dissect and analyze them. We should compare these two experiences. The kind of feeling we should seek to arouse in the children is: Unfortunately we have to dissect nature when we bring it into the classroom. But the children should nevertheless feel this as a necessity, for the destruction of what is natural is also necessary in the building up of the human being. We should certainly not imagine that we are doing any good by giving a scientific explanation of a beetle out of doors in natural surroundings. The scientific description of the beetle belongs in the classroom! When we take the children out into the open we have to arouse in them delight at the sight of the beetle, delight in the way he runs about, in his drollness, delight in his relationship to the rest of nature.

Furthermore we should not neglect to call forth in the child's soul a clear sense of how something creative lies in music, something transcending nature, and of how man himself shares in the creation of nature when he develops music. This will be formed as a feeling only very primitively of course, but it will be the first that must emerge from the element of music—that the human being feels himself within the cosmos![44]

Knowledge of the human being

As director of the school, Steiner had deep relationships with his teachers and pupils. He saw in their eyes what they needed and answered their questions. His responses came not only in conferences and daily conversations but also in approximately two hundred lectures on education. In each of these supplementary lectures he included new insights into our *knowledge of the human being*.

Steiner introduced his insights in the morning lectures for the first teachers, now known in the English language as *The Foundations of Human Experience*. Some of these ideas spilled into the afternoon lectures when he also presented *educational principles, methods* and *exercises for teachers*. In the first afternoon lecture he set the tone for all of our work: "We have to realize that in employing our method we shall be dealing in a particular way with the harmonizing of the higher man, the spirit and soul, with the physical, bodily nature, the lower man."[45]

We use the subjects to develop the child's soul and physical forces in the right way. We use knowledge to develop human capabilities. Therefore we need to distinguish between subject matter that is conventional and knowledge that is based on universal human nature.

Sympathy and antipathy

Steiner introduced the role of sympathy and antipathy in his methods, especially when he gave practical advice on working with speech.

Sense activity is really a limb activity in which sympathy holds sway while antipathy comes forth from the nervous system. When sense perceptions enter the head, the nervous system is interrupted. This interruption is based on antipathy from the child. The child uses antipathy to understand the sense perceptions. The same is true of the act of seeing. Sight comes about when sympathy in the blood vessels in the eye meets the antipathy in the nervous system of the eye.

Both forces also meet in the child's chest where their whole being is active. If a child becomes scared, he reacts immediately. His instincts send reflexes into the subconscious that are mirrored in the brain, in the soul, and create a picture element.

In the child's chest a sympathetic activity interacts continually with a cosmic activity of antipathy. These activities unite in human speech. We understand speech when the meeting of antipathy and sympathy in the chest is accompanied by the brain. In the chest it is more real, in the brain it fades into an image. Speaking and feeling rest on the constant rhythm of sympathetic and antipathetic activity.

Steiner described how speech is rooted in human feeling; all that the individual brings to the world from his own feeling of astonishment meets the cosmic relationship in the vowel 'O.' The feeling we have of emptiness is related in 'U.' The feeling of admiration is expressed in 'A.' The feeling of offering resistance is expressed in 'E.' The feeling of approaching and becoming one with something is found in 'I.' Vowels express inner soul moods.

When we bring consonants to meet the vowels, we provide antipathy. Our tongue, our lips, our palate make themselves organs of antipathy.

Steiner considered speech as a genuine synthesis in the child of the music with the plastic element. Vowels encompass something musical while consonants encompass something sculptural. Once again both streams of art appear as the source of the artistic element for all of our teaching.

Exercises for teachers

One of the biggest problems I met while teaching in America is the gap between the experts on education and the people who do the teaching. I know experts with PhDs on the most important aspects of teaching who have little or no daily experience in the classroom with children. I also know teachers who do not feel entitled to researching their own work, for they are to carry out the plan and methods created by the so-called experts and approved by the politicians.

In addition politicians and businessmen, with no experience in the classroom, assume the right to be experts in education in the name of democracy. The right connections are not being made between teacher and child. Methods are not effective. Vast human and financial capital is being wasted on systems that do not meet the needs of our children.

Why exercises for teachers? They provide methods for bridging the gap between adults and children. Only when we learn to change and grow can our children discover our growth as human beings. When they notice us changing, they also may be inspired to change. The thoughts a teacher brings into the classroom not only provide more effective teaching but also are the source of a possible spiritual relationship between the teacher and the children.

Steiner gave his first teachers practical advice on how to bring the right attitude into the classroom. To achieve inner connections with the children and then enable the children to develop their interest for the world out of their own being, the teacher can practice an understanding of himself as part of the cosmos and not just as a person limited to the classroom.

Much depends on the nature of the teacher's feelings towards the growing child, and how much we can really revere the growing human being in the child, as a mysterious revelation of the cosmos. Very much depends on the teacher's ability to develop this feeling in his own life. Then he can more powerfully revere it in the children he works with.

As usual Steiner does not tell teachers how to do the exercises. Steiner merely suggests it is totally up to the individual to take the initiative and try out what works for him. In lecture two he helps the teacher broaden his perspective by looking into the relationship between breaths taken each day and the Platonic year, which is the cosmic revolution of the sun.

The human being takes about 18 breaths a minute. In four minutes this is 72 breaths. In one day it is $18 \times 60 \times 24 = 25{,}920$ breaths per day. Or we could take the number of breaths in four minutes, 72. Instead of multiplying 24×60, I can multiply 6×60 and get 360. Then 360 days $\times$ 72 breaths is also 25,920 per day.

Our breathing is a miniature of what the sun does each year. Steiner poses the question: What is sleeping? In waking and sleeping we also breathe something in and out. When we go to sleep, we breathe out our astral body and our self and we breathe them in every time we wake up. In one year we complete something similar to what we complete each day. If we live roughly 72 years and we multiply that with 360 to find how many days we have breathed our astral bodies and self in and out, we have again 25,920 times. Now we have two breathing processes, each day and each year.

A third breathing process follows the course of the sun. During 25,920 years the sun moves gradually around the ecliptic in one planetary cosmic year. Our individual breathing process is an image of the great cosmic process.

"Overcome the illusion that you are a limited human being; conceive of yourself as a process in the cosmos, which is a reality, and you will be able to say: I am myself a breath drawn by the universe."[46]

Exercise for teachers #2

Here the goal is to better understand the child's inward life of feeling. This is her mood of soul. People shy away from such observations because they do not like infringing upon others. Yet teachers are in the classroom every day with children who have a certain mood. The children want to be seen.

To improve the ability of understanding their mood, Steiner suggested we practice by observing the soul life of a person whom we have known for some time, who has recently died. We can ask what was the state of his soul six years ago? We take everything into account that we know of him and find that his soul mood six years ago already had, unconsciously playing into it, the preparation for the death he was soon to meet. It played unconsciously into his feeling life at that time, his mood of soul. A person who is soon to die has quite a different mood of soul from one who still has long to live.

You begin by creating a clear picture of the state of soul someone had in the past. You form a picture of the mood of soul of the person by selecting some of the things he produced that year. You ask: What played into his soul life in that year? Then you look at what happened from his birth to the year you have selected. And then you look at everything from that year until the person's death.

Steiner used his understanding of Goethe as an example. In the year 1790 his soul was filled with a combination of what was to come later, as well as what he had already experienced.

"A teacher must be able to regard life more profoundly, otherwise he will never succeed in handling the growing human being in an appropriate and productive way."[47] This is important. We can learn to see our children in new ways. We dare ask ourselves what their mood of soul may be. We try to understand what has been in the past and also what may unfold in the future. This helps us meet them more deeply in the daily work. The next time we see them we may see something new!

Sources

All quotations are from *Practical Advice to Teachers*, Rudolf Steiner, Stuttgart, August 21 to September 5, 1919, GA 294, Rudolf Steiner Press, 1976. (Typographer's note: Quotation marks have been omitted from much of the material from Steiner's lectures for readability. All sections are duly referenced in these endnotes.)

Educational Principles:
1. Lecture One, August 21, 1919, page 9
2. Lecture One, August 21, 1919, page 17
3. Lecture Two, August 22, 1919, page 39
4. Lecture Three, August 23, 1919, page 40
5. Lecture Five, August 25, 1919, page 74
6. Lecture Five, August 25, 1919, page 75
7. Lecture Five, August 25, 1919, page 83
8. Lecture Six, August 26, 1919, pages 88 and 89
9. Lecture Six, August 26, 1919, page 90
10. Lecture Thirteen, September 4, 1919, page 177

Methods
11. Lecture Four, August 24, 1919, pages 55–60
12. Lecture Four, page 61
13. Lecture Three, page 47
14. Lecture One, page 21
15. Lecture Four, page 61
16. Lecture Thirteen, page 180
17. Lecture Three, pages 48–51
18. Lecture Three, page 52

19. Lecture One, page 21
20. Lecture Four, page 66
21. Lecture Four, page 62
22. Lecture Six, page 93
23. Lecture Six, page 94
24. Lecture Six, page 94
25. Lecture Six, page 89
26. Lecture Four, page 69
27. Lecture Five, page 71
28. Lecture Five, page 73
29. Lecture One, page 14
30. Lecture One, page 16
31. Lecture One, page 16
32. Lecture Two, page 30
33. Lecture Two, page 32
34. Lecture Five, page 76
35. Lecture Five, page 77
36. Lecture Five, page 78
37. Lecture Four, page 64
38. Lecture Thirteen, page 181
39. Lecture Thirteen, page 184
40. Lecture Five, page 82
41. Lecture Thirteen, page 183
42. Lecture One, page 24
43. Lecture Thirteen, page 179
44. Lecture Three, Page 53

Knowledge of the Human Being
45. Lecture One, page 9

Exercises for Teachers
46. Lecture Two, page 36
47. Lecture Six, page 92

What Was That? Forgetting and Remembering

by Albert Schmelzer
translated by Genie Sakaguchi

One of the most popular imaginations of the learning process is the picture of the Nürnberg Funnel. It's placed on the head of the student, and then the prepared knowledge is poured in bit by bit. Unfortunately, this practical device has a catch, which we know from our everyday experience: forgetting.

> *Yesterday I still knew the twenty new English vocabulary words,*
> *and today five have blown right out of my head!*

Is forgetting the enemy of learning? Should we direct all our pedagogical efforts to the end that students have as complete a memory as possible? Whoever concerns himself with research into learning and memory will quickly note that it is not so simple. There are people who can hold the words from twelve thousand books in their heads but cannot dress themselves, or those who know all the powers to the fiftieth power of all two-digit numbers, but remain behind in middle school. Such "idiot savants" often purchase their fantastic memory with lower intelligence in other fields and with deficits in the emotional or social realm. One woman complained about her capacity to remember immediate experiences from her personal life or a political event in connection with every date of the year. Every day her whole life runs through her head and makes her crazy.

Imagine what it would be like not to remember.

Obviously it is important for every pedagogical practice to take into consideration why we need memory and what form of memory we are striving for. Imagine that we could not remember. Experiences would flow by, and everything in every moment would be unusual and new. We ourselves would be a blank page; consciousness would split into as many splinters as there are moments, but also that which makes us a personality would fall apart. Memory gives us the possibility of learning: Discoveries can be remembered and passed on, and to be able to bring what is past into the present creates the precondition for shaping the future. The meaning that memory has for us will become clearer if we consider the various forms of memory, as differentiated by science today, such as short-term and long-term memory.

A first, elementary stage of memory is the so-called "priming": Stimuli that were taken in earlier and then are met with again are inculcated more deeply into the memory. Television commercials take advantage of this; first a long spot is used, followed by a slightly different, shorter variation later.

A second type of memory is procedural memory, which includes capacities such as swimming and riding a bicycle, as well as playing a musical instrument.

The pure, context-free memory of facts can be considered a third stage. This would include facts such as: "Paris is the capital of France" and "The Thirty Years' War took place between 1618 and 1648."

The highest form of memory, but also the one most susceptible to disturbances, is the episodic-autobiographical memory. This enables us to travel in time back into the past, to bring specific events in our own biography and also historical happenings into the present—something like factual memory permeated with reflection.

As one considers these various forms of memory, it becomes clear on the one hand that we need all of them, and on the other hand, it makes sense to say that forgetting is to be regarded not as the enemy, but rather as the necessary polarity of remembering. For what would it be like if the painstaking process of learning to swim or learning to write were constantly remembered and brought into consciousness? It is important that once certain things are learned, they sink into unconsciousness. Through forgetting we build capacities. This holds true not only for forms of movement but also for cognitive processes: Practicing arithmetic problems, writing essays, doing foreign language exercises all lead to the effect that certain processes penetrate our "flesh and blood" and now as accomplishments stand at our disposal.

Forgetting also has meaning for the episodic-autobiographical memory: It creates space for experiences to be processed and woven together with other experiences and leads one to the essence of events. According to memory researcher Hans-Joachim Markowitsch, forgetting is much less the disintegration and disappearance of information that has been received, and much more the adjustment, downgrading, and reshaping of what had been acquired earlier.

Memory is not a hard disk.

This formation of memory shows that in old age the experiences of childhood can be remembered more colorfully than events of the preceding decades, that we lighten negative experiences with high spirits, and conversely, we suppress unimportant aspects, so that we do not drown under the burden of a glut of information. In this sense Honoré de Balzac said, "Memory brings beauty to life, but only forgetting makes it bearable."

The dynamic and subjective nature of remembering shows that the oft-repeated comparison with the computer is mistaken. There is no place in the brain that is a "hard disk" site having the name of memory, no particular region for short-term or long-term memory. In spite of intensive investigation, there is still no clear answer to the question about the bodily anchoring of memory. While thirty years ago one used the analogy of the card index of an old-fashioned library, with each area of the brain corresponding to a specific function, now a reversal has taken place—going so far as to say that a particular region of the brain, relevant to the particular representation of an experience, can change over time or with increased practice of a capacity.

Remembering means waking up, forgetting means going to sleep.

A good memory, as should be clear from our considerations about forgetting, is not necessarily a complete memory, but rather one that consists of a healthy rhythm between forgetting and remembering. Rudolf Steiner spoke of this as early as 1919, in the lectures now published as *The Foundations of Human Experience* [also known as *Study of Man*]. In these lectures Steiner connected the interaction between forgetting and remembering to the rhythm of sleeping and waking. Steiner said, "What is remembering? It is the awakening of a constellation of ideas. And what is forgetting? The going to sleep of the constellation of ideas."

Such a conceptual formulation opens up an interesting perspective. Self-observation and sleep research both show that sound sleep leads to bodily recuperation, balance in the soul, and a stronger presence of the "I." Sound sleep fosters spiritual presence and enables us to react more quickly and more appropriately in the face of the unexpected. Correspondingly, can we therefore say that forgetting enables fresh learning? This question leads to the field of pedagogy. It is necessary to describe the conditions that lead to a good memory.

Remembering requires attentiveness and emotion.

To begin with, it is important to observe how new impressions and content are taken in. In general one can say that something will be remembered well which is received with keen attention, energetic interest and, above all, an intense involvement of the feelings. Who does not remember his first love? The emotions build "the unchanging, constant core of the memory organization," according to psychologist David Rapaport. Rudolf Steiner characterized the feeling life as the actual "bearer of the constant imagination."

The interdependence of the efficiency of the memory with the degree of attentiveness and emotional involvement has, since that time, been experimentally demonstrated. From this arises the first pedagogical requirement: The curriculum should alternate between moments of concentration and relaxation. It should be structured in a lively and pictorial way; in short, it should be immersed in the medium of the artistic. Where it is possible, it will be helpful to take into consideration the affinity between rhythm and memory. The ancient Greeks knew what an aid a particular poetic measure could provide to the memory: *The Iliad* and *The Odyssey* were understood to be the curriculum and were learned by heart. The ongoing effect of such a rhythmical memory is particularly impressive when the rhythmical element is supported by movement. Rhythmical stomping and clapping facilitate learning the times tables, and rhythmical movement in connection with metrical verses or rhymes helps acquire foreign languages.

Memory needs movement.

The reference to the element of movement brings up a further topic that has meaning for the education of memory: Will activity creates a sound basis for remembering something. For this reason, it is good, in the study of biology for example, not only to look at the various forms of plants, but also to draw them. Or in language classes, it is important to practice dialogue, role-playing and little scenes. It appears that the important thing is that an inner participation is aroused. The ideal would be to describe an historical figure so vividly that a picture is inwardly built up and the person's experiences can be felt with inner empathy.

This will-directed memory formation actually has roots in history. In earlier times nomadic tribes would erect monuments at the places where something important took place. When they returned to these places, the past experiences would arise again. We can experience a kind of reflection of this "local memory" still today when we visit the places of our childhood after a long absence, perhaps even wander around a bit, and then note what a wealth of memories suddenly arise. It has been noted how feelings and will activities can be connected with the acquisition of new material, to facilitate remembering later.

Learning is consolidated in sleep.

Now we can return to the important, above-mentioned productive role of forgetting. "Active forgetting" takes place, for example, in healthy sleep. Sigmund Freud, in his book, *The Meaning of Dreams* (1900), spoke of the importance of sleep for processing the impressions of daily life. Since that time, numerous studies have shown that insufficient sleep, or lack of opportunity for particular periods of sleep—such as REM sleep, or deep sleep—leads to gaps in memory. Sleep has a very important meaning for the consolidation and individualization of impressions, facts, and other content taken in during the day.

These facts provide the decisive foundation for organizing the curriculum in Waldorf pedagogy. It is set up so that the introduction of a new topic does not lead to a conclusion on the first day. Rather, on the first day the interest is awakened, attention is guided, and the feelings and will of the student are called upon. This happens, for example, with a physical experiment that is carefully observed and appreciated with wonder, after which it is followed by the unconscious processing that takes place during the night. When the lesson is taken up again the next morning, it is presented in a way that it answers the need that has arisen in the students for classification and penetration of the material with thoughts. The lesson guides the working out of concepts and laws pertaining to the phenomena. This threefold ordering of the lessons, arranged with the participation of will activity, involvement of the feeling life, and conceptual penetration over two days, is one way in which forgetting can be integrated into the lesson plan. Another way (of taking advantage of forgetting) is to use polarity in the alternation of subjects in the main lesson blocks: When a particular subject is allowed to sink into forgetfulness, the essential points can be brought out when the theme comes up again at a later time and incorporated into the students' individual experiences.

Learning in three steps

After the receiving of information and the processing of it, there follows remembering. The success of this step has to do with the strength of the already-mentioned factors that an individual has at his disposal at any give point in time. Everyone knows that this strength is not just a question of conscious motivation. Many times, even with the best will, we cannot come up with what we are trying to remember, although we feel that the name, the event, or the connection is right on the tip of our tongue. The strength to bring what has sunk down into unconsciousness back to conscious awareness depends on the entire life organization, above all psychological and physical health. When a child is nervous or sick, he will not be able to remember things well. Stress and anxiety are counterproductive to all stages of memory formation and function. Psychiatry is familiar with countless varieties of stress-induced disturbances of the memory. Stress can lead to blocks which bar access to information.

With these considerations it appears that a curriculum that can do without pressure and threats of failure, in the place of which the learning process is penetrated with a pictorial quality, imagination, and humor, is the best training for memory, and more meaningful than the Nürnberg Funnel.

LITERATURE

Hans-Joachim Markowitsch. *Dem Gedächtnis auf der Spur. Von Erinnern und Vergessen*, Darmstadt 2002.

Rudolf Steiner. *Allgemeine Menschenkunde als Grundlage der Pädagogik*, 7. Und 8. Vortrag, Dornach 1992.

_____. *The Foundations of Human Experience*, also published as *Study of Man*.

_____. *Menschenerkenntnis und Unterrichtsgestaltung*, 1. Vortrag, Dornach 1959.

David Rapaport. *Gefühl und Erinnerung*, Frankfurt a. M. 1997.

Manfred Spitzer. *Lernen. Gehirnforschung und die Schule des Lebens*, München 2007.

Brought to the School by the Police?

by Henning Köhler
translated by Ted Warren

> *Never give in. Force the children to school no matter what. Use medicine, the police or pills. This is serious.*

In a *Spiegel* Online-Interview, the leading German SPD politician, Sigmar Gabriel tried to use the "Sarrazin-Effect" for his own purposes. Thilo Sarrazin's book, *Deutschland Schafft Sich Ab,* proposes expulsion if the foreigner's will to integrate is missing and threatens to use the police to do so. For example, if immigrant children do not attend school.

But it is difficult for the police to pick up a Turkish child who skips school and not a German. That is too stupid! Gabriel must allow justice to reign within his threats. Whoever does not send his children to school consistently and on time, whether he is German or an immigrant, "We will send over the police and you will pay the fine." As so often in our beautiful, new world, the maxim for crisis management is threat rather than cooperation. As if that is how we will resolve the integration problem!

In order to control more of the suspected or actual black sheep, Gabriel wants to sharpen mandatory school attendance to the point of including tardiness as deserving of punishment. For him tardiness is so important that children, in case of an emergency, should be brought to school by the police. Recently there was an article in the German medical periodical, *Deutschen Arzteblatt*, concerning fear of school. The tone of the article was to never give in, force the children to school no matter what. Let us remember the following facts:

In most European countries there is not mandatory school but rather mandatory education.

According to the United Nations Convention on Children's Rights, all parents may decide which type of education they want their children to experience. This privilege is removed only if the parents lose their right to parenting.

School today is a leading pathological factor in the childhood years. Responsible parents have the duty to seriously consider whether or not they want to send their children to school.

Critical experts in education doubt whether "the school arrangement is the right prerequisite for educating human beings." (Ursula Germann-Mueller)

Rather than perfecting the imposed school system, should we not take an example from Denmark? There almost anyone can start a school with very few bureaucratic regulations, even in their own living room. The government takes on 80% of the costs. This model works. A study showed recently that in Denmark the world's most satisfied people live. Is there a correlation here?

Forty years ago a priest Ivan Illich became famous due to his appeal in the book, *Entschulung der Gesellschaft (Deschooling Society)*. Today we experience a repressive trend towards total "schooling" of our children's lives. How the times have changed. Slowly a new movement is emerging. Here is some literature for interested parents:

Andre Stern: *Und ich war nie in der Schule. Geschichte eines glücklichen Kindes*
   [And I was never in school. The story of a happy child.]
Johannes Heimrath (editor): *Die Entfesselung der Kreativitet. Das menschenrecht auf Schulverweigerung.* [Unleashing creativity: The human rights on truancy]

Short but fine contributions.

Elemental Beings Are Real for Many Children

Conversation with Katharina Dreher-Thiel
translated by Genie Sakaguchi

It is not only Waldorf Kindergartens that are populated by dwarves, elves, and gnomes. Many classic children's books such as *The Root Children* by Sibylle von Olfers and *Children of the Forest* by Elsa Beskow enjoy uninterrupted popularity despite opposition from rational thinking. From research in child development we know that for children all things and beings, especially in nature, are alive. The following is a conversation between a staff member of the journal, *Erziehungskunst*, and Katharina Dreher-Thiel, a class teacher of many years' experience, and now a support teacher (*Förderlehrerin*) at the Free Waldorf School of Bad Nauheim, about her dealings with nature spirits in her lessons.

Interviewer: Why is the perception of elemental beings (nature spirits) more than childish animism?

Katharina Dreher-Thiel: Because there really are nature spirits in the etheric world. Others knew this besides Rudolf Steiner. Many people of earlier cultural epochs, up until the 15th or 16th century, were able to perceive nature spirits. This capacity disappeared more and more with the beginning of modern times and our rational way of thinking. We have preserved the remembrance of these beings of the etheric world like a collective memory in our fairy tales and sagas. Today it appears that the ability to perceive the etheric world, and interest in nature spirits, is growing again.

Interviewer: Do dwarves, elves, and other beings still have a role to play in the lower grades?

KDT: Yes. In the narrative material of the lower grades—the fairy tales, sagas, and meaningful stories—they play a very central role. These wonderful pictures fulfill an important task: They "nourish" and structure the soul being of the child. Children always open up with joy to these elemental beings, so one can use them to carry pedagogical material. This works, however, only when the knitted dwarves on the classroom's seasonal table are not gathering dust, but rather, are involved in and allowed to live through rituals and routines in the lessons.

Interviewer: How far is the children's relationship to the elemental world taken into account in the lesson plans?

KDT: Young children live strongly in their environment and are much more connected with it than adults are. In this dreamy consciousness, the figures of the fairy tales and sagas live, and with appropriate openness it is possible for children to perceive the elemental beings. This condition of consciousness continues to have an effect in the First and Second Grades. The lesson plans take this fact into account through the artistic methods of teaching, whereby the picture-forming capacities play an especially important role, for example in the introduction of the letters through pictures. A further central factor is the already-mentioned narrative material.

Interviewer: Do the children speak of their "supersensible" perceptions?

KDT: Seldom. These perceptions are not supersensible for them, but rather, real experiences. Moreover, they often discover that they cannot speak with adults about these things. I once had the great good fortune to have an open conversation on this topic with my Seventh Grade class. Shame-faced and with a chuckle, they told about experiences from their childhood: young girls who had played with elves in a flowering meadow, and one young boy who, while having a high fever, saw his guardian angel and spoke with him.

Interviewer: What are the reasons why these capacities are lost in later stages of life?

KDT: The feeling-impressions that the children have experienced through the fairy tales and stories sink down and are forgotten, but they continue to work on, building and structuring the children's soul-life. Many children lose the capacity to see nature spirits around the age of nine or ten, when they gain some distance from the environment and develop a more wakeful consciousness for the sense world. Others at this same age become aware of the special nature of their perceptions and continue to interact with these beings as a matter of course—at least, that is what Waldorf students have told me—in the past and today. I think that in the face of the increasing intellectual demands of the upper grades, spiritual perceptions fade into the background, or perhaps disappear altogether. In adulthood, however, these perceptive capacities can come alive again. These capacities are lost earlier, the less they are "nourished" or encouraged.

Interviewer: When cute dwarves and rough hobgoblins lose their attraction, how does the teacher awaken the feeling for nature spirits?

KDT: Through teaching that is pictorial, artistic and full of imagination, in which the themes of the lessons are characterized in a lively way. When plants, animals, personalities and historical times, chemical elements and physical laws are characterized with all their special aspects in a lively manner, and brought as a soul experience, then the students sense, unconsciously, that nature is alive in its essential being.

Laughing with the Ninth Graders

Humor in the Main Lesson

by Florian Heinzmann
translated by Genie Sakaguchi

In Waldorf schools in Grade Nine the so-called Humor main lesson block is taught. This has a serious background. For just at this age young people need a capacity that allows them to see themselves with other eyes. The German teacher, Florian Heinzmann, gives an idea of how it might go.

Steffi and Corinne stand in front of the class, leading a panel discussion of "experts." The moderators seat their guests in front of a "running camera," in front of the public. There are a few conditions: All contributions follow in alphabetical order: The first begins with the letter A, the next with B, and so on.

Steffi begins: "So, dear members of our audience, a heart-felt welcome to the Monday Morning Show, where the theme today is, Hammer Throwing Competition in Hawaii. How do you feel so soon before the contest, Mrs. Schneider?" – "Very well, thank you, very well." "Cholesterol problems are not allowed to occur here in Hawaii, am I right?" – "I believe that is so. The food in our hotel is absolutely excellent." – "Iron deficiency? Do the competitors here often suffer from iron deficiency?" – "Perhaps, oops, sorry, Fanta is good for this condition."

The themes were chosen by students, according to my guidelines: We need some kind of sport and an exotic land. The students laughed, and the actors did, too. The exercise came from the Improvisational Theatre, an independent art form established some years ago, founded by Keith Johnstone and spreading around the world, becoming a box-office hit. Like the exercise mentioned, there are many exercises from improv theater that are very practicable for school use. One can divide the students into groups of two to four students (two moderators and two interviewees), and let them practice on their own. At the end, the courageous ones can perform before the whole class.

A good Humor main lesson is one where there is a lot of laughter. And this is, naturally, true for other main lessons as well. Every student learns best when the instruction is fun, and the instruction is fun when it's full of humor. In this respect the Humor main lesson is perhaps the best practice for good teaching. And in addition, laughter is not only healthy, but it also trains the thinking. [In German, the word for "joke," *Witz*, comes from the word for "knowledge," *Wissen*.] There is a quote from Goethe's *Faust*: "A comedian could teach a preacher." Not for nothing do comedians count as reliable and dependable advisors, as recognized in the great success of Hape Kerkeling's book describing his experiences on the Camino de Santiago.* Improtheater is a reliable stimulator of the laugh-muscles. I use these exercises every morning in the rhythmical section of my Humor main lesson, and not only in the Humor main lesson. I see improtheater as a sustainable alternative to choral speaking. It might even be the salvation of the rhythmical part of main lessons overall.

Great humorists serve as stimulation.

In the first five to seven days of the Humor main lesson block, we take up various humorous texts. Here, above all, my goal is to move the students to engage in creative writing or other artistic forms.

We read or listen to sketches from comedians such as Loriot, Rüdiger Hoffmann and Horst Schlämmer, and then act them out in groups. We tell many jokes, both teacher and students—without sex, violence, or disrespect to human beings—and write poems in the styles of Christian Morgenstern, Kurt Tucholski, Joachim Ringelnatz, Ernst Jandl, Heinz Erhard and Erich Kästner. One can have the students write a poem in the style of the original, and with a similar title. [There is an example here, built on word-play, that would be very difficult to recreate in English. The original poems presented were "Ottos Mops" by Ernst Jandl and the subsequent student's poem.]

---

*Published in English as *I'm Off Then: Losing and Finding Myself on the Camino de Santiago*, by Hape Kerkeling, 2009.

As with all teaching, it is recommended here as well to be as close as possible to the spirit of the times and one way to do that is to use contemporary texts. Robert Gernhardt, Ror Wolf and Thomas Gsella can be drawn upon, for example. Just as tragedy is oriented towards what is high and noble, in the essence of humor there is a certain element of coarseness or earthiness. The weaknesses of human beings and their gross physicality are essential characteristics of all comedy and should therefore also be allowed to be themes.

Further we discuss and draw appropriate cartoons from current events reported in newspaper articles. We read funny short stories, such as "Der Filialleiter" ["The Branch Manager"] by Thomas Hürlimann, and we also write funny stories. The introduction for this can be a comical or puzzling picture from a magazine, for which the students supply an explanation in their story. A favorite creative assignment is composing a parody of a fairy tale in the style of Ringelnatz's "Rotkäppchen" ["Red Riding Hood"]. We discuss irony and sarcasm in such examples of satirical graphics from Klaus Staeck or something from the magazine, *Titanic*. In these cases one must choose carefully to avoid offending sensitive students. In addition, students can make their own satirical collages with items from magazines. Especially, in connection with this project, the students need to clearly understand that the goal of satire is not to hurt people, but rather it serves to bring up, in a mocking manner, deplorable conditions in the social life or cases of a lack of virtue.

The deeper meaning of the Humor main lesson block

In the second part of the main lesson block, we take up a longer prose text, for example, "Schischiphusch," by Wolfgang Borchert, or a comedy. The time for Zuckmeier's "Hauptmann von Köpenick" ["The Captain from Köpenick"] is unfortunately past. The comedy as well as the deep symbolism in Kleist's "Der Zerbrochene Krug" ["The Broken Pitcher"] would scarcely be understandable for a Ninth Grader. Shakespeare's comedies (*A Midsummer Night's Dream*, for example) are by far and away more accessible for students. Unfortunately good and equally deep comedies in post-war literature are rare, especially in German literature. One unavoidably lands in the Theatre of the Absurd (for example, Beckett's *Waiting for Godot* or Ionescu's *Exit the King*) or in tragic-comedy (such as Dürrenmatt's *The Physicists* or *The Visit*). This last piece is actually meant for Grade Nine like no other. For one thing, the close connection between tragedy and humor can be discussed and rated as a symptom of the times, and secondly, there arises a new aspect of comedy, namely, black humor.

Yet it is not only this. The mixing of tragedy and humor corresponds to the nature of humor in general: There is always a depth, a truth, and a seriousness, as one can discover in the character, temperament, and biography of all clowns and all genuine comedians. And it corresponds to the feeling life of the Ninth Graders, who find themselves in an uncertain stage between childhood and adulthood, through the onset of puberty.

Deep longing for hilarity

With the increase of hormones that often goes along with a distancing from the parents, the soul life of the Ninth Grader is often marked by swings of mood and feelings. Laughing and crying lie nearer to each other than perhaps ever before—and closer than they will ever be again in life. A deep longing for hilarity goes hand in hand with an inner abyss of vulnerability. For all these reasons, the theme of humor, together with the second German main lesson block of Grade Nine, the Goethe-Schiller Block, in which, naturally, the theme of tragedy predominates, works in a healing and balancing manner on the soul of the Ninth Grader. Through this the students should learn what in the ordinary course of events they cannot yet do: to laugh at themselves. This heightened distance to the self is an important part of individuation on the path to a healthy self-consciousness. This is also helped by drama, and attending dramatic performances is important as well. But the high point of the Humor block for me is attending a comedy or other humorous play. Also, professional improvisational theatre pieces and theatrical competitions can be recommended in this regard, and are much enjoyed by the students.

The Humor block is a great opportunity for every upper grades teacher who is suddenly in front of a new Ninth Grade class, as yet unknown to him. Humor lends itself, as almost nothing else, to the forming of social relationships: "Laughter is not the worst beginning of a friendship, and it is by far the best end." (Oscar Wilde, *The Picture of Dorian Gray*) And so I was not really surprised when a student asked me after the Humor block was over, "Will we have a Humor block again in Grade Ten?"

LITERATURE

Marianne-Miami Andersen: *Theatersport und Improtheater,* Planegg, 1996.
Christoph Göpfert: *Jugend und Literatur*, Stuttgart, 1993
Malte Schuchardt: *Lachen und Weinen. Humor und Tragik in Kunst und Literatur*, Stuttgart 2005.

www.ingramcontent.com/pod-product-compliance
Lightning Source LLC
Chambersburg PA
CBHW040016240426
43664CB00038B/26